A Ragged Mountain Press
WOMAN'S GUIDE

SCUBA DIVING

CLAIRE WALTER

Series Editor, Molly Mulhern Gross

RAGGED MOUNTAIN PRESS / McGRAW-HILL

Camden, Maine • New York • San Francisco • Washington, D.C. • Auckland
Bogotá • Caracas • Lisbon • London • Madrid • Mexico City • Milan
Montreal • New Delhi • San Juan • Singapore • Sydney • Tokyo • Toronto

Look for these other Ragged Mountain Press Woman's Guides

Backpacking, Adrienne Hall

Canoeing, Laurie Gullion

Climbing, Shelley Presson

Fly-Fishing, Dana Rikimaru

Golf, Susan Comolli

Mountaineering, Andrea Gabbard

Snowboarding, Julia Carlson

Powerboating, Sandy Lindsey

Sailing, Doris Colgate

Sea Kayaking, Shelley Johnson

Skiing, Maggie Loring

Winter Sports, Iseult Devlin

● ●

Ragged Mountain Press
A Division of The McGraw·Hill Companies

10 9 8 7 6 5 4 3 2 1

Copyright © 2000 Claire Walter

All rights reserved. The publisher takes no responsibility for the use of any of the materials or methods described in this book, nor for the products thereof. The name "Ragged Mountain Press" and the Ragged Mountain Press logo are trademarks of The McGraw-Hill Companies. Printed in the United States of America.

Library of Congress Cataloging-in-Publication Data

Walter, Claire.
    Scuba Diving / Claire Walter.
        p.   cm.—(A Ragged Mountain Press woman's guide)
    Includes bibliographical references and index.
    ISBN 0-07-135138-8 (alk. paper)
    1. Scuba diving. 2. Women divers. I. Title.
        II. Series

GV838.672.W35 2000
797.2'3—dc21   00-021502

Questions regarding the content of this book should be addressed to
Ragged Mountain Press
P.O. Box 220
Camden, ME 04843
http://www.raggedmountainpress.com

Questions regarding the ordering of this book should be addressed to
The McGraw-Hill Companies
Customer Service Department
P.O. Box 547
Blacklick, OH 43004
Retail customers: 1-800-262-4729
Bookstores: 1-800-722-4726

This book is printed on 70# Citation.

Printed by Quebecor Printing Company, Fairfield, PA
Design by Carol Inouye, Inkstone Communications Design
Illustrations by Elayne Sears
Production management by Janet Robbins
Page layout by Shannon Thomas
Edited by Constance Burt

Aqua-Lung, Band-Aid, Cyalume, Dramamine, Hookah, Little Xtra, LubeSuit, Lycra, Polartec, SafeAir, SASY, ScubaPro, Sea-Bands, SlapStrap, SNUBA, Spare Air, Sudafed, Vaseline, and Velcro are registered trademarks.

Photos courtesy the author unless otherwise noted: pages 35, 41, and 100, courtesy Aqua-Lung; page 123 courtesy Tom Campbell/ Adventure Photo; page 32 (left) courtesy Dacor; pages 21–22, and 120 courtesy Wayne Hassan; page 86 courtesy Al Hornsby/Outside Images; page 96 (top left) courtesy IkeLite; pages 29 and 99 courtesy Index Stock; page 37 courtesy Island Dive and Water Sports/ Rosario Resort, Orcas Island WA; pages 45–46, 49, 72, 74, 93, 95, 106, and 110 (top), courtesy Mark Krohn; pages 31, 65, 71, 76–77, and 115, courtesy Warren F. Miller; page 105 (left), courtesy Monterey Bay Aquarium; pages 18, 40, 90, 96 (top right), 102, and 108, courtesy National Oceanic and Atmospheric Association; page 34 courtesy Oceanic; page 88 courtesy PADI; page 82 courtesy Palau Visitors Authority; pages 14–16, 25, 42, 44, 64, and 98 (top), courtesy Linda Reeves; page 32 (right) courtesy ScubaPro; page 96 (bottom left) courtesy SeaLife; page 104 courtesy Paul Sutherland/ Shark Research Institute; page 39 courtesy Tusa; pages 11, 60, and 73, courtesy Michael Verdure/ScubaPro; pages 28, 75, 85, 98 (bottom), 105 (right), 112, 122, and 129, courtesy Norbert Wu; and page 110 (bottom) courtesy www.arttoday.com.

....

"Diving is the only religious
experience I've had. It's the
only place where I can really
see God—quite clearly."

—Lauren Hutton, model, actress,
and environmentalist

....

CONTENTS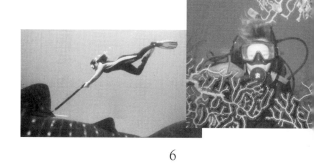

 **CONTENTS**

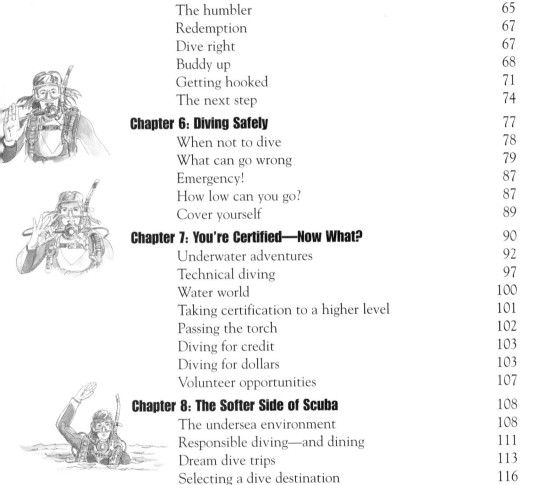

Acknowledgments

Many thanks to all the divers and people in the dive industry who shared their thoughts, experiences, and insights with me. Patty Newell-Motara, publisher of *Women Underwater* and Jennifer King and Lorraine Bemis-Sadler of the Women's Scuba Association and the Women's Equipment Test Team were generous with their time and insights. They took the time to review the equipment chapter, for which I am especially grateful. Without Marion Rivman, former public relations counsel for the Diving Equipment and Marketing Association, and Steve Weaver of Weaver's Dive Center in Boulder, Colorado, my dive career and therefore this book would not exist. I am grateful also to Lisa DeYoung for her research assistance. She'll be a certified diver before this book comes off press. My deepest gratitude goes to Molly Mulhern for creating this long-needed series of books on active sports for women. She and her colleagues at Ragged Mountain Press have helped make this book as good as it is. And thanks, as always, go to my husband Ral Sandberg, my favorite dive buddy.

Introduction

I dive because I love to ski, I dive because I live in Colorado, and I dive because I once snorkeled Australia's Great Barrier Reef. These may seem an odd combination of reasons, but perhaps when I explain them they will be as clear to you as they were compelling to me. A similar set of feelings or experiences may have stirred your interest in diving, too.

When it comes to sports, skiing is my first passion—and to me, skiing and scuba diving are the "same sport," but in totally different environments. Both are equipment-intensive. You can't ski without skis, boots, poles, protective eyewear, and ski clothing, and you can't dive without a buoyancy compensator, compressed-air tank and regulator for breathing, mask, snorkel, fins, and, usually, some kind of specialized garment. Both are individual sports yet extremely sociable activities. In diving, the aspect of being "un-alone" is mandatory underwater; in fact, the buddy system has been canonized.

The social aspect carries over to topside life too. These two sports attract the same kinds of people. Divers and skiers alike take their sports seriously but also enjoy socializing at the end of the day, swapping tales, comparing notes, toasting to great times both past and future. While many people can ski or dive close to home and do so, the travel component is important in both sports. But most important, diving, like skiing, is done in a beautiful natural environment.

I also dive because I am a Connecticut native who now lives in Colorado and no longer takes the proximity of salt water for granted. I've never been enraptured by swimming pools and have a take-it-or-leave-it (usually leave-it) attitude toward swimming in lakes. But saltwater is something else. I love its smell and the way it feels against my skin. The sound of waves and the ocean's tidal rhythm are pleasing to my ears. I moved to Colorado in 1988, and I soon realized that living a thousand miles from the nearest ocean means that I have to travel for my saltwater fix. When I dive, I immerse myself in salt water, and that holds me for a while. Diving also provides a reason to travel to islands and coastal communities known for their beautiful scuba diving sites. Great places to dive are a real getaway from the equally beautiful snow-capped mountains that now comprise the framework of my life.

And I dive because one sublime day of snorkeling on the Great Barrier Reef persuaded me that I wanted to be a participant in the subaquatic world, not merely a spectator. Snorkeling is fun and the sights can be truly wonderful, but snorkelers tend to paddle along on the surface, looking down at the action. Divers truly immerse themselves in the marine environment, and that's what I wanted to do.

WHAT IS DIVING?

Well before the development of mechanisms that allowed humans to breathe underwater, people dived into shallow seas to harvest the ocean's bounty. Sponge divers in the Mediterranean and the female pearl divers of Japan were able to stay underwater on one breath long enough to bring their aquatic harvest from the seafloor. In the years just before World War II, rudimentary recreational skin diving appeared. Divers wore primitive fins, homemade snorkels, and masks, which at that time were called goggles. In fact, these pioneers, who remained close to the surface and relied on their own lung capacity, were called *goggle divers.*

Technological advances soon enabled divers to stay underwater longer than one single breath. Military divers began to use a limited underwater supply of pure oxygen, good only to about 30 feet; commercial deep-sea divers donned heavy full-body suits, brass helmets, and long air hoses connected to a shipboard air source. Like flying, diving freely without being tethered to an air source long languished in the imaginations of the adventurous.

In 1943, a French naval officer named Jacques-Yves Cousteau changed diving forever. He developed the Aqua-Lung, a compressed-air source enabling divers to stay underwater far longer and dive deeper, thus turning imagination into reality. His haunting and incredibly beautiful photographs of what had until then been a secret and hidden environment inspired many people to want to share the experience. Also at that time, the U.S. Navy was training "frogmen" as an underwater tactical force. Fast-forward to *Sea Hunt,* a postwar television series in which actor Lloyd Bridges starred as Mike Nelson, an underwater action hero engaged in weekly aquatic adventures.

When recreational scuba diving became feasible, women as well as men were captivated by it. However, the physical requirements, drawn from Navy training for young men who had already survived boot camp, were impossible for most women—full-body pushups while wearing scuba gear, for example. But some gutsy women persevered.

"I've been certified since 1962—in a college class, in Miami," recalls Yvette Cardozo, a native Floridian now living in Issaquah, Washington, and still diving. "It was me, 30 hormonal 18-year-old boys, and a lot of very large knives. That was back in the Mike Nelson underwater-knife-fight era. Very interesting, especially since the instructor truly thought women should be banished to another universe."

Women weren't banished—on the contrary. Our certification numbers, especially as entry-level divers, have increased steadily, and the Women's Scuba Association (WSA) (for contact information, see chapter 10, Resources) was created to promote and support women in diving. As our numbers have grown, the kinder side of scuba has developed too: women-specific products have appeared on the market and nobody needs to do full-body pushups to become a diver.

WHO DIVES?

It's almost easier to point to who *doesn't* dive than who *does.* Young children don't dive because certifying agencies require people to be at least 12 years old for junior certification and 15 for full certification. Only recently has limited dive instruction become available for children aged 8 to 12. According to 1998 statistics, there are 8.5 million certified divers in the United States. Certification is valid for life, but this does not mean that every diver is active—or that every one who is active dives every year. In fact, the Diving Equipment and Marketing Association (see chapter 10, Resources), scuba's trade association, estimates that 2.4 million Americans dive every year. They represent all walks of life, a great range of ages, and a wide geographic distribution.

According to the Professional Association of Diving Instructors (PADI, see chapter 10, Resources), which certifies a considerable majority of new divers (approximately 70 percent of that 8.5 million), 38 percent of the nation's certified divers are married, half have college degrees, nearly two thirds are between 25 and 44 years old, 39 percent are in a professional or managerial occupation, and 28 percent are female. The proportion of women to men is growing slowly but steadily. For every woman who is deterred by the ratio, feeling that she will be outnumbered and perhaps condescended to on every dive, there's at least one other woman who looks at those statistics and decides that diving is a good way to meet men.

"I met my husband in the British Virgin Islands," says my friend Judy Wade, who lives in Phoenix, when I told her about writing this book. "If you want stories about underwater kisses and hand-holding while gliding through a school of brilliantly colored parrotfish, I can give you a few. Bill is an instructor trainer and had the patience to show me how to see things underwater that I'd been missing for years." In fact, diving is an excellent coed activity that couples enjoy together; people on very different athletic planes on land are closer to equal underwater. But many women prefer to dive with other women.

For more than a decade, California and Florida, with their huge populations and long coastlines, have alternated as the one-two states in terms of annual PADI certifications, followed by Texas, New York, and Illinois. Landlocked Colorado, with about 4 million residents, has ranked number six since 1994, making it the state with the highest number of certified divers in proportion to population. Georgia, Hawaii, Massachusetts, New Jersey, North Carolina, Ohio, Pennsylvania, and Washington have rounded out the top 10 in PADI certifications in various years. If you live in one of these states, it should be especially easy to find a nearby dive shop and diving companions.

ABOUT THIS BOOK

Diving takes place in an environment that is as intrinsically hostile to humans as outer space. Technology enables us to function, to some degree, in both places. In the case of diving, newcomers to the sport must become familiar with water's effects on the body, the equipment that enables us to adapt to that environment, and the fundamentals of dive technique. This knowledge is not optional and it isn't something that you pick up along the way.

Unlike the vast majority of other recreational activities, scuba diving is not something you simply go out and learn on your own. Learning from a friend isn't wise, either. Rather, you must undergo training and take a test to ensure that you have learned the fundamentals of being a safe diver. You must assimilate a fairly large body of knowledge before you pass the test, earn your scuba certification (which is explained in detail in chapter 4), and call yourself a diver. The entire process is somewhat complicated, and this book is designed to demystify scuba diving by sorting out its intricacies.

As you begin your dive training, remember that there will be times when what you need to learn about physiology, equipment, and scuba diving's rules of the road may seem overwhelming. Don't be discouraged: every bit of knowledge brings you closer to accessing that magical undersea world.

Chapter 1

WOMEN AND SCUBA DIVING

Diving appeals to women with different levels of sociability, adventure, athletic skill, technical interest, physical courage, and aesthetic sense. Some dive because they can enjoy the camaraderie of other women with similar interests. Some dive because it's an escape to another realm that they can do close to home; for others, like me, diving provides a reason to travel to distant shores. Some like the image of strength and athleticism that diving projects. Others are enamored with diving because they like the physical sensation of weightlessness and enjoy breathing *compressed air*. Such diehards will dive in any waters, any time. Some people (OK, mostly guys) are gearheads who are really into the equipment aspect of the sport and spend more time reading dive magazine test reports and new-product news than gazing longingly at photos of exotic travel destinations.

Diving attracts jocks-to-the-core who are driven to challenge themselves all the time. They are of the type who train for marathons, try to lift more weight in the gym, or see how many ski runs they can take in a day. As divers, these folks pile skill upon skill, collecting *certification cards* that represent new notches. They view advanced-level *technical diving* as something of a trophy. By contrast, some people thrive underwater because scuba diving provides freedom of movement, even for those with mobility impairments or poor physical conditioning. Others dive because of the sheer beauty of the marine world and their fascination with the critters who inhabit it. And that's the main appeal to me.

HALL OF FAME

Women have made enough of a splash in the scuba world that a Women Divers Hall of Fame was created in 2000, honoring 70 influential women divers. They include Zale Parry, costar of the legendary *Sea Hunt* television series; Dr. Sylvia Earle, America's preeminent marine biologist who was former head of the National Oceanographic and Atmospheric Administration and now the National Geographic Society's explorer-in-residence; cave diver Jill Heinerth; free-diver Tanya Streeter; editor and writer Bonnie Cardone, and dive industry leaders who have championed the development of women's equipment and who have pioneered a place for women in the ranks of professional diving.

"**W**hat woman wouldn't jump at the chance to feel weightless? Diving is the perfect sport. You do it lying down, you don't sweat, nothing sags, and when you stop kicking, nothing bad happens— and the scenery is still great."

—Dale Leatherman, Snowshoe, West Virginia

A SPORT FOR (ALMOST) ALL

Diving is a sport for virtually every healthy adult. It crosses the lines of gender, age, and physical fitness. After all, everyone is naturally buoyant in water—runners with minimal body fat and overweight people alike. It's a sport that even many physically challenged people can enjoy, and several organizations are devoted to introducing them to the exhilaration of diving.

Anyone old enough to remember *Sea Hunt*, a television hit (1957–61) starring the late Lloyd Bridges as underwater adventurer Mike Nelson, knows that it inspired thousands of people to dream about diving. Although Zale Parry had a featured role and was an early role model for women divers, scuba diving was definitely a guy's sport in Mike Nelson's fictitious world. That notion, however, is as obsolete as the black-and-white celluloid with which it was filmed. Men still outnumber women in the diving community, but it's a sport where women also excel. Diving requires neither extraordinary strength nor an exceptional level of fitness, although every physical activity is easier and more pleasurable if you're in reasonably good shape.

Good health is also a bonus, but many conditions do not preclude diving. Much research has been done and empirical evidence has been collected on who can dive and what special precautions might be necessary. It's important to alert your dive instructor to any physical problem you have so that he or she will be prepared and ready to respond appropriately if required. Brute strength is not an issue for most divers because dive pros and boat crews help handle the gear. *Tanks* and *weight belts*, which seem so cumbersome on land, are not so underwater.

THE MANY FACES OF SCUBA DIVING

A range of aquatic activities falls under the general category of scuba diving. Snorkeling, the simplest of them, is not diving at all, while the most complicated is highly technical diving. Snorkeling is the easiest element of the scuba-diving continuum. It takes no particular training and a minimum of equipment—*fins* to help you move across the water, a *mask* so that you can see, and, of course, the *snorkel*, a mouthpiece and *tube* so that you can breathe while swimming facedown in the water. When a snorkeler inhales and submerges underwater, then comes up for the next breath, that is known as *skin diving*. This is today's version of the goggle diving of yore (see page 8).

Scuba diving involves using equipment that enables you to breathe underwater (see chapter 3). You can sample diving to see if you're drawn to it or you can take a short course that will prepare you to take a guided shallow dive. Once you decide that you're serious about diving, you will sign up for a full course that will lead to *certification*, which in turn will enable you to join a dive trip. Higher levels of certification are available for those who want greater adventure or even a career in diving (see chapter 7).

Women come to diving for various reasons, and the ages and circumstances of those who have taken to the water are also wide-ranging. Mia Persad, managing director of Footprints Eco Resort on the southern Caribbean island of Tobago, says she was virtually raised in the water. "One of my earliest memories is hanging on to the side of the pool, kicking," she recalls. "I must have been about three. As a teenager, I spent as much time in the water as on land and used to have recurring dreams of being underwater. I remember hiding underwater, and I knew I'd be safe if I could stay there, so I held my breath as long as I could. Diving is like an extension of that dream for me."

For Annemarie Leon, an artist who grew up in Australia, the dream was more of a nightmare. Her father drowned when she was three, and as an adult now living in Boulder, Colorado, she recognizes that her way of overcoming her father's death was to make herself comfortable underwater.

Like many women, Holly Johnson of Lafayette, Colorado, started diving because of a guy. "I wouldn't be married if I didn't dive," she says. "For our first Christmas together, Perry bought me dive lessons and a starter set of equipment. I got certified at the Blue Hole [a quarry in northern New Mexico], where I saw one fish in this murky water and was ecstatic. He said to himself, 'She's hooked!' He planned our whole engagement around my first dive trip to Marsh Harbor in the Bahamas. Now we have a rule: it's the one thing we can't do without each other. He can go

• •

"**P**eople frequently have a problem that has chopped into their self-esteem—
losing a job, going through a divorce, or something. When they become
proficient at something they thought was impossible, it helps in so many ways.
They move through a fearful process to feel confident in the water."

—Ellen Holland Keller, YMCA Scuba, Cleveland, Ohio

• •

Women dive for a variety of reasons, including as a triumph over some kind of adversity. For most, however, the beauty of the underwater environment is prime.

• •

"**O**f course women should dive. After all, half of the creatures underwater are female."

—Dr. Sylvia Earle, marine biologist, author, and National Geographic Society explorer-in-residence

• •

fishing or golfing without me and I can run marathons without him, but we dive together."

For others, diving is simply a way of life. Leslie Robbins grew up in Florida, where her family had its own *dive boat*. Her dad was the family *divemaster*, filling the tanks from an onboard compressor and setting up everyone's gear except Leslie's, because she preferred to handle her own. Then, once when he was not aboard, "I became the temporary divemaster," she says. "My mother isn't strong enough to lift a tank and my husband tends to get seasick. I had to set up all the gear."

For Chris Nugent of Arvada, Colorado, the revelation came relatively late in life. "My husband and I went on a cruise for our 30th anniversary," she says. "We saw divers while we were snorkeling, and we decided to try it. I got certified when I was 49, and we've been diving together for 15 years. We had shared kids, a home, a life, but we had never shared a hobby until we started diving. It gives purpose to our travels. Since my hair turned gray, I often feel that younger people look through older people. But when we dive, we communicate and that feeling goes away. That doesn't happen on any other kind of trip." She has since retired from her position as a legal secretary and now works part-time running the office at Weaver's Dive Center in Boulder, where she was certified, to help support her dive habit.

Whatever your reasons for and concerns about learning to dive, others have jumped into the water before you: young women and gray-haired grandmas; brave women who easily rise to physical challenges and timid women who had to overcome their fears; women who struggled and sacrificed financially to dive and women for whom diving is a trivial expense; and lithe, toned athletes and sedentary women for whom diving was their first athletic endeavor.

Women who dive

The sometime-snorkeler

Frances, a 40-something homemaker from suburban Chicago, doesn't much care for the water, but she goes snorkeling when she and her family vacation where the sea is warm and the sights close to shore are worth seeing. Her husband is an avid fisherman. Because no one else in the family shares his passion, she and the children rent snorkeling equipment and paddle around. She loves the children's excitement at seeing fish underwater. Frances is reassured by the safety of calm, shallow water and she has no real desire to learn how to dive—although her 14-year-old daughter Jenny is angling for a dive course when she gets older.

The resort diver

Margie, a single career woman in her mid-30s, and several of her women friends from the Washington, D.C., area take a tropical vacation every year. On a lark, they signed up for a resort course a few years ago. For Margie, casual diving is quite enough. She enjoys the feeling of being underwater, but she's content to follow an instructor and then stretch out on a chaise with a piña colada and a good book. She has now returned to law school, so diving a little and relaxing a lot are her idea of a great tropical vacation. Her friend Meredith, on the other hand, got her scuba certification a few years ago, when she was dating a man who was a passionate diver.

The aficionado

Meredith's start in diving was as casual as Margie's, but she fell in love with both a man who dives and the sport of diving. By the time she got her certification, she was hooked. She and her boyfriend took a dive vacation each year of the three years they were together, and Meredith's underwater knowledge increased. When the relationship ended, Meredith kept diving. She has rejoined her women friends on their annual tropical vacation, but she always signs up for the more serious diving adventures available at the resorts they visit.

The mover

Sandra was a fast-track New York career woman who began diving in much the same way as Margie and Meredith. However, when her company was taken over by another and her position was eliminated, she sublet her apartment and used her severance pay to rent a condominium in the Virgin Islands for six months. She found a part-time job in a dive shop to decompress from her corporate life, and quickly worked on her advanced certification levels. She's never going back to her old life. Now in her late 30s, Sandra is about to become a dive instructor and wants to open her own dive shop someday. She returned briefly to New York to get rid of her old apartment and donate her dress-for-success outfits and black cocktail dresses to charity. And, oh yes, she's had an octopus tattooed on her ankle.

The natural splendor of the subaquatic environment ranks at the top of the motivations women have for diving. Here, a diver peers into an underwater cave.

UNDERWATER EXPERIENCES
· · · · · · · · · · · · · · · · · · ·

Here's a progression of underwater experiences, from being a passenger on a tourist submarine ride to truly technical diving:

- **Underwater submarines.** Tourist rides at depths of up to 100 feet. You won't even get wet!
- **Tethered diving.** Called SNUBA, Hookah, or similar terms, these activities are available in a few tourist destinations. While underwater, you breathe through a *regulator* attached to a compressed-air source on the surface.
- **Discover diving or introduction to diving.** A little basic theory and a chance to try scuba gear underwater, usually in a pool.
- **Resort course.** A fundamental course that usually begins with a pool session to get used to the equipment, followed by a guided shallow dive.
- **Certified diver.** Certification as a scuba diver, which enables you to dive independently (i.e., with a *buddy*, rather

(continued on next page)

Half of a twosome

Jean and Ed, both in their 50s, have been diving for more than 25 years. Long ago, when they were courting, they discovered that they had both been teenage *Sea Hunt* fans, and when learning to dive was practical, they did it. Dive trips have been an important part of their vacations. They are veterans, as comfortable with each other underwater as they are in the rest of their lives. They are both educators, so they take their dive vacations when school is out. Their college-age children were certified as soon as they were able, and the family still books its annual trip with the local dive shop. They plan to continue diving forever but, in her most private thoughts, Jean can't imagine diving if Ed isn't with her.

The pro

Terry grew up in southern California, where her youth was defined by the sand, the sun, and the surf. As a troubled teenager, she fell in with a rough crowd, becoming involved with drugs, alcohol, and a parade of disreputable friends. At one point, she learned to scuba dive on a dare. The familiar ocean, seen from a

new perspective, turned Terry's life around. Diving in the magical underwater kelp forests of Catalina Island was transformational. She cleaned up her act and moved to Hawaii, where she quickly became a dive instructor. At age 28, she married a professional underwater photographer. Together they own a dive boat and sell beautiful undersea art photography.

The adventure begins as soon as a diver is underwater, whether or not the sights are dramatic.

The scientist

Growing up in Montana, Karen always knew that she wanted to be a scientist. A serendipitous educational track led her to Seattle and to marine biology. Now in her late 30s, she has her Ph.D. and a position with an educational and environmental organization concerned with the marine life of Puget Sound. She spends time in the water and in the laboratory. She is a cold-water diver whose passion for the deep has never abated.

What these women and all of us share is an appreciation of the underwater world, with its incomparable beauty and its combination of resilience and fragility.

BUT IS IT EXERCISE?

Is it like running? No. Like aggressively swimming laps? No. Like mountain biking uphill? No. Like a kick-boxing class? No. But is diving an active, aerobic sport? Yes. Unless you're hovering in the water to study a small section of reef, diving requires constant activity. You swim during the descent and underwater, and when you have dive gear on your back before entering the water, you certainly are involved in a weight-bearing activity. It takes additional energy when you're swimming against the current, aggressively kicking your fins, heavily weighted, or diving in cold water. According to Rodale Publications, which issues both *Scuba Diving* and *Prevention* magazines (see chapter 10, Resources), the more a diver weighs, the more energy expended during a dive. Not bad for such a beautiful activity!

UNDERWATER EXPERIENCES
• • • • • • • • • • • • • • • • • •

(continued from previous page)

than following an instructor), go on dive trips, rent dive gear, and even have your own tanks filled.

• **Specialty and advanced levels of certification.** Everything from Advanced Open-Water Diver to Instructor courses. Different levels are available from various *certifying agencies.*

• **Commercial diving.** Hard-core career diving, often in challenging water and weather conditions, such as working on an offshore oil rig, bridge construction, and emergency rescue underwater. Military diving is also career diving, but with a tactical orientation.

Chapter 2

GETTING STARTED

T he image of gliding weightlessly through the water, flirting with fish, cavorting with dolphins, and exploring a magical underwater world appeals to many women. Scuba diving is the means to such a fantastic end. It combines structure and freedom, and every step in your diving experience will reinforce this. Some experts believe that women are often the best divers—eager to learn properly, respectful of the hazards, appreciative of the aesthetics, and conscientious about the maritime environment.

Diving is different from other activities in that even the most adventurous people don't simply go out and do it. It isn't a teach-yourself-from-a-book or learn-from-a-friend sport. While there are instructional aids, such as manuals, tapes, and even CD-ROMs, nothing replaces personal instruction. The instructor doesn't only teach but also monitors what you have learned. At the end of any dive course, the instructor tests your proficiency, both in theory and in the water.

There is a valid reason for this. *Safe* is the most important adjective that can be attached to the noun *diving*. Safety requires structure. You will find structure built into the learning process and structure in every dive you ever make. To be a safe diver, a beginner needs to master a specific set of underwater *skills*. A professional dive instructor helps you learn those skills and tests you to see that you possess them. When you have completed your first course, you will be officially certified as a scuba diver. The entire process of getting certified follows a very specific path, from the most cursory introduction to the intricacies of technical diving for those who continue on.

There also is structure in the form of rituals performed before every dive: pairing up with a buddy; checking your own equipment; checking each other's equipment; listening to the briefing from an instructor, divemaster, or guide; and planning your dive within the parameters outlined in the briefing. Don't feel hemmed in by all of this, for the structure is designed to make you as safe as possible. As paradoxical as it might sound, only by diving safely, knowing your limits, and being conservative can you feel the freedom of the sport and enjoy the matchless beauty under the surface of the sea.

> "I went to San Carlos, Mexico, for a weekend. Not being one to sit on the beach, I borrowed a snorkel and didn't get out of the water for a week. Now, I dive."
>
> —Mary Peachin, Tucson, Arizona

TESTING THE WATERS

Because would-be divers don't know how it feels to be underwater and how they will respond to this alien environment, many local dive shops and tropical resorts offer scuba's equivalent of the test drive. However, instead of driving around the block and kicking the tires, you get to try on scuba gear and do a supervised dive in a shallow swimming pool. Like a test drive, such one-session programs—called Discover Scuba, Introduction to Scuba, or something similar—are free or nominally priced. I know of one big dive shop in Michigan that refers to each Introduction to Scuba program it offers as a "Splash Party" to convey scuba's feeling of fun and frolic.

No matter what it's called, this single session puts you at the threshold of a beguiling and exciting activity. You will feel the thrill of weightlessness and perhaps the natural high that many people get from breathing compressed air while underwater—all under close supervision and in the safety of a pool. The month of June is promoted as National Scuba Month and is a good time to keep an eye open for an exploratory program at a convenient site.

The risks of trying before you buy are few and the rewards are many. The instructor begins with a brief orientation of scuba equipment and the basics on how to use it. The most important aspect is the opportunity to actually try diving. And how tantalizing it is! Some people find out quickly that they are extremely uncomfortable, even claustrophobic; this is an easy way to determine whether they think they can overcome the discomfort or that diving is not for them. If you're already intrigued by diving and your first underwater experience is a good one, the odds are that you'll sign up for a full course right there, and within a few weeks, you'll have earned your certification card.

SIGNING UP

If the instructor in charge of your trial run is particularly congenial, find out if he or she will be teaching a basic course at a convenient time for you and sign up. Otherwise, whether you sign up with a local dive operator or while you're on vacation, you take potluck on who your instructor

ISN'T DIVING DIFFICULT?

Here's a test to see if you've got what it takes: Fill your bathtub with water, pinch your nose, close your eyes, and duck your head under. No panic? You'll do fine.

—Premier issue (Jan./Feb. 1999) of *New Diver*, a Rodale Press Publication

"**I** was exhilarated and soothed by the sound of my own breath. I breathed deeply and exhaled fully because I loved the sensation of coming up and sinking a little with every breath. I immediately yearned to see more underwater than my fellow inductees and the occasional Band-Aid at the bottom of the pool. I signed up for a class practically before I had dried off."

—Sarah Wilson, Hartford, Connecticut

will be. Find out who will be teaching when you want to take the class and talk to the instructor before signing up. You can probably tell rather quickly whether the chemistry between you is good, and you can also ask about specifics of teaching style. Women-only classes, taught by female instructors, are offered periodically by a few dive centers. If you're interested, inquire—or form a group of female friends who want to learn to dive and set up a custom-class just for yourselves.

There are no standards for personality or teaching style, but in every other matter of qualification, you can feel confident that everyone who teaches diving has met certain standards. Each certifying agency trains and certifies instructors who, in turn, train and certify divers. Instructors must adhere to certain standards and have passed specific tests to be qualified to teach diving. Likewise, divemasters have become competent with a certain skill set. Any dive center that takes the risk of hiring an unqualified instructor—which is highly unlikely—is inviting serious liability consequences. PADI (see the next section), the largest certifying agency, has a system called Pro-Check, where you can check the current status of any instructor on the PADI roster by calling a toll-free number.

AGENCIES FROM A (ACSU) TO Y (YMCA)

Divers are constantly throwing acronyms into the conversational air: PADI, NAUI, SSI, and others. The folks in the dive shop talk about DEMA too. There's an entire alphabet soup of organizations in diving. Who are they and what do they do?

Let's start with the easy one: DEMA, the acronym for the Diving Equipment and Marketing Association. This trade association organizes the sport's annual trade show, which the crew from your local dive shop is likely to attend as buyers. The vendors include a hodgepodge of equipment, divewear, and accessory suppliers (i.e., manufacturers, importers, and distributors); certifying agencies; travel suppliers (i.e., dive resorts, airlines, and state, local, and foreign tourist boards); dive-related book and periodical publishers; and all sorts of specialized businesses and organizations looking for a presence in the dive industry.

No matter which training agency you sign up with, you'll learn to use scuba gear. Junior certification is available from age 12 up, with full certification possible for 15-year-olds and older.

The alphabet soup of certifying agencies seems much more confusing (see chapter 10, Resources, for a list of agencies operating in North America). Whether you sign up locally or while on vacation, the dive shop you go to will use the curriculum and training aids from one or more of these agencies. You may wonder if it's better to have a PADI card, a National Association of Underwater Instructors (NAUI) card, or a Scuba Schools International (SSI) card—or whether you ought to sign up for the scuba class at the YMCA or YWCA, where you learned to swim as a youngster. In addition to diving instruction, the Y emphasizes *watermanship*, an awkward word used to describe a very useful skill set. Survival floating, swimming underwater, and various snorkeling maneuvers are among the skills that are not necessary for diving. However, some experts believe that the confidence in water that develops from practicing them helps build a better diver. In reality, most people don't choose an agency when they start diving; rather, they select a congenial and convenient dive shop and go with its program, no matter what its acronym. Especially at the entry level, the knowledge and skills that the courses cover are quite similar.

No matter which agency you go with, you will be laying the foundation on which to build a life of diving. The names of programs and courses offered vary somewhat among agencies, but regardless of the acronym, you will learn to use your gear and the importance of safe diving. When you've mastered the skills and passed the tests, you achieve your first goal: earning the certification card, or *C-card*, that will identify you as having demonstrated fundamental diving know-how. Depending on the organization, this level might be called Open-Water Diver, Open-Water Scuba Diver, Scuba Diver, Skin Diver, or something similar. This small card is your passport to diving. It will enable you to join dive trips, rent scuba gear, and get your tank filled for independent diving.

Just remember that, with the exception of the not-for-profit YMCA, all agencies are businesses, out to make money. Think of them as wholesalers of dive training. They sell educational material, books, videos, T-shirts, and other paraphernalia to dive shops and dive resorts, which

Children can be certified from age 12. Most diving instruction, for both children and adults, begins in a pool.

are the industry's retailers. And you're the customer—the target market. Every certifying agency or organization acts as if its program is the best. In fact, the differences are subtle, perhaps even cosmetic, because certifying agencies belong to an umbrella organization called the Recreational Scuba Training Council, which meets annually to create the standards of training and safety that enable the dive industry to thrive and grow. Entry-level programs are quite similar.

WHAT WILL IT COST?

The most accurate answer is, "It depends." However, assuming that you learn to dive locally, expect to pay an average of $300 a course. This covers classroom and pool time, course materials (e.g., the instruction manual and dive tables), most equipment used during the course, and your *open-water* check-out dives, which you can think of as the final exams of your early diving education. Convenient home- or independent-study options are available from some agencies, but convenience carries a price—such a course can cost more than learning the theory in the traditional classroom setting.

Most instructors are paid by the dive shop or resort where they are employed, but some are independent and paid directly by students. If you find a course advertised for much less, you may have to pay separately for the instructor's time, the check-out dives, or some other important component—or, you may have lucked out on a really good promotion offered by a local dive shop.

We talk in detail about gear in chapter 3 but here's a summary of equipment and costs. Virtually all dive training centers supply the *buoyancy compensator* (BC), regulator, tank, and *weights* for their classes, but they generally charge extra for the *wetsuit* rental, which is often needed for the open-water dive. Students usually must provide their own mask ($30–$150), snorkel ($15–$50), and fins ($50–$175). You can rent this equipment, but most beginners choose to purchase it right away. You can go one of two ways: start with low-end gear and figure that you'll trade up when you really get into the sport, or spend more for higher-performance gear and know that it will accommodate your requirements as your skills improve and interest grows—and they will.

"**W**hen I lived in Florida, I didn't dive. I had friends who did, and I thought that they were crazy. But then another non-diver and I bumped into a two-for-one sale at a dive shop—and I was hooked."

—Martha Slonim, Colorado Springs, Colorado

SHORTCUTS

Other than some certifying agencies' option of home or independent study for the theoretical portion of a course sequence, there are no real shortcuts to becoming a fully certified Open-Water Diver, which you will eventually need if you want to dive a lot. However, there are shortcuts if you just want to dive a little. If you aren't a diver but would like to be, just a few hours' training focuses directly on dive skills and allows you to sample the underwater world.

A class of beginning divers prepares to make its first excursion into the waters of Aurora Reservoir in Colorado. Instead of offering a Resort Course, local dive operators joke that they offer a Reservoir Course to introduce newcomers to the sport.

Many tropical resorts offer a one-day introduction usually called Resort Course or something similar, and some cruise lines offer a similar program, with the first practice dive in the ship's pool, followed by a guided *shore dive* at one of the ports of call. Such a course is not too time-consuming or technical, but neither is it so superficial that you don't get the thrill of open-water diving.

PADI has gone a giant step farther and now offers what can be described as "precertification certification," called Scuba Diver. It begins with three sessions in the swimming pool to familiarize the group with the equipment—much like the try-before-you-buy programs—followed by two well-supervised and guided dives in shallow open water. The course also includes the first three modules (i.e., chapters) from PADI's Open-Water Diver course. What this largest of certifying agencies has started, others will probably soon follow.

Actually, Club Med should be credited with the concept of short-cutting the formerly lengthy certification process. Because people typically spend just a week at a Club Med tropical resort, years ago the club created its own scuba course, which required less book-learning and allowed new divers to get underwater quickly, in carefully controlled situations. This initially caused much distress among mainline certifying agencies, which at the time were still tethered to the old mode of navy-based diving. But for simple recreational diving, it works—as the current proliferation of similar resort courses indicates.

Club Med's program and other agencies' resort courses begin with the fundamentals, first in the pool and then in the sea. At Club Med, if you combine two days of instruction with four days of diving with an instructor, you get a special certification card that lets you dive at a Club Med resort anywhere in the world.

You may be one of the many divers who have completed a resort course and are happy to dive that way, vacation after vacation. Or you might be so smitten by the experience that you will want to add the more theoretical aspects of the sport taught under the PADI, NAUI, SSI, or other system to get your certification.

DEEP-SIX THOSE FEARS

Okay, you're not claustrophobic, you have a sense of adventure that lures you to the deep, and you don't have any medical problems—but still, something is stopping you from diving. That "something" could be one niggling concern, or perhaps a whole quiver of fears, about what might befall you underwater—or even before you get into the water. Here are some common concerns and the answers that will perhaps help you put those fears to rest:

- **"I can't afford to dive."** Divers will tell you that you can't afford *not* to dive, because the sport is worth every penny. In terms of equipment outlay, diving is on a par with such passions as downhill skiing and golf. If you plan to dive a lot, you'll amortize that quickly, but if you aren't sure of your diving future or know that you will dive only occasionally, approximately $150 for a mask, snorkel, and fins will get you started. You can rent everything else from a dive shop or at a dive resort whenever you need it. Rental prices vary considerably among dive destinations.

- **"I'm not a good swimmer."** Divers don't need to be super-swimmers, and many are not. Being comfortable in the water is far more important than great form or speed. Many fine, experienced divers are neither stylish nor fast swimmers. To get certified, you will need to swim a specific distance in a pool and float or tread water for a specified amount of time.

- **"I'm not technically inclined, so I'll never be able to pass the course."** Most certifying agencies have honed their introductory courses to the material that new divers, who typically dive in supervised situations, need to become comfortable and safe in the water. The curriculum is paced in a logical step-by-step progression, and the instruction manuals and audiovisual aids are clear. Classes include theory, but they focus on the basics of what you need to know. *Confined-water* training in the pool is performance-based, so you learn about your equipment step by step. The final training dives are usually held in shallow open water. In addition, some agencies now have an introductory or limited certification program for those who don't want to get involved in technicalities and who plan to dive only under the close supervision of a dive pro.

- **"Diving is dangerous. I might even die."** Yes, you could die, but the possibility is statistically very remote. When recreational divers adhere to set protocols and dive conservatively, particularly in a controlled and supervised setting, diving is one of the safest of all "adventure sports." According to the National Underwater Accident Data Center and the Divers Alert Network (DAN), the ratio of fatalities to dives has decreased by more than half since the late 1980s. In 1996, for instance, DAN reported only 85 fatalities in a population of

The beauty and fascination of the ocean realm chase many new divers' fears away. So does the thorough training required for certification.

approximately 2.4 million divers who made 17 million dives. Of those deaths, nearly 20 percent occurred during extremely advanced dives (including in deep and complex underwater caverns), which you're highly unlikely ever to make.

- **"I'm afraid that I won't be able to breathe."** The most complicated part of all that scuba gear is there so that you *can* breathe underwater, and there is built-in redundancy as a backup to ensure safe diving. The main thing to remember is to watch your pressure gauge so that you don't use up all the air in your tank before you reach the surface. During each pre-dive briefing, the dive instructor, divemaster, or guide will tell you at what point it's time to surface.

- **"I've seen *Jaws*—a shark will get me."** People eat infinitely more sea critters than sea critters eat people. Sharks have occasionally been known to attack humans, but the victims are more likely to be shore-hugging surfers or swimmers than gear-laden divers out in open water. More important, most sharks that divers meet are shy species that would rather not get too close to humans. If you see sharks, don't poke, pester, or provoke them, and they'll extend you the same courtesy. The most aggressive species are the great white sharks, found along Australia's southern coast and in a few sections off northern California— and even they are rarely encountered. Also consider that shark dives, with or without protective cages for divers, are gaining in popularity. These thrilling encounters would not be promoted if the sharks attacked the clients.

- **"Can I dive while I have my period? Will sharks smell blood in the water and attack me?"** There have been few shark attacks on divers in general, fewer on women, and no data suggest that sharks go after menstruating women.

However, some evidence exists that women are at slightly greater risk of *decompression illness* (DCI) or injury while they are menstruating, perhaps because fluid retention and swollen tissue make the body less efficient at getting rid of dissolved nitrogen. The answer is to dive more conservatively to decrease this risk.

- **"What about birth-control pills?"** Oral contraceptives might also contribute to DCI, so conservative diving—meaning shorter, shallower, and/or fewer dives, and/or longer safety stops—is a good idea.

- **"What do I do about my contact lenses?"** You can wear contact lenses, whether soft or rigid gas-permeable, with your mask. The pressure exerted by the water will not press the lenses into your eyeballs. However, the dehydration that diving causes will dry your eyes, so be sure to bring some rewetting solution to use after each dive. The major concern involving contact lenses comes while you're learning your skills (see page 61). One of the skills involves taking your mask off and putting it back on underwater, which contact-lens-wearers find difficult because a contact lens could wash out. Keep your eyes closed as you remove your mask and keep them closed until you have repositioned your mask and cleared the water out of it.

- **"I wear dentures."** Whether due to vanity or habit, most divers keep their alternative teeth in, especially if it's a partial denture held securely with clasps. Lower dentures are more easily displaced than uppers, which could cause a breathing obstruction. Some divers remove their dentures, in which case a custom mouthpiece is safer and more comfortable than an off-the-shelf model.

- **"I'll get lost underwater."** It's a fact that humans cannot see as far underwater as they can topside, and the combination of moving in a two-plane rather than a three-plane world, weightlessness, currents, and the absence of familiar landmarks is disorienting. New divers are wise to stay with the dive guide, who not only makes sure everyone gets back to the boat, but also points out interesting formations and critters. Try to buddy-up with an experienced diver, and be sure to orient yourself before you head away from the dive boat. Learn to use a compass and bone up on underwater navigation skills so that you can return to the boat's *descent line* or anchor line, even on a night dive. (These skills are part of advanced scuba courses.) Also remember that while your field of vision is limited underwater, the boat captain and his helper can see all the divers' bubbles breaking the surface. On a *drift dive*, you float with the current; when the dive is over and you pop up to the surface, the boat picks you up.

- **"What about the bends?"** *The bends* is dive jargon for *decompression sickness* (DCS) or *decompression illness* (DCI), which can happen when a diver descends

ADDRESSING FEAR

"I was trained as a nurse and got really involved in geriatric care. Then I fell in love with diving, and eventually said to myself, 'I'm an educator.' I went back to Barry University and, at 35, was one of the first two graduates to get a degree in sport management in the dive industry. I've set up an education program and built a career on helping people with fears about diving.

"These fears can be addressed by one-on-one contact. When you know what the fears are, you can iden-tify what to do in order to work around them to reach a goal. Sometimes it's as simple as going to a corner of the pool and practicing a skill. You can take someone to the shallow end and say, 'If you're having trouble, all you have to do is stand up.' That brings security.

"If a student says, 'I know I'm having a little problem with this skill. Give me a little space to practice,' I know she will keep up good underwater communication. She'll stay in contact with me. The mark of a good instructor is to respect that individual's style and hang back.

"As an instructor, you might have to break each skill down minutely. Say that mask-clearing is difficult for a student diver. I teach them to crack the mask a little and clear; then a little more and clear; then full flood and clear. It usually works. It's a lot like cooking. We cook something and change it a little at a time until we get the result we want.

"Women are great adapters. They'll say, 'Let me try that again.' In the end, women make better divers. They have strong observational skills. They're good at deductive thinking should an emergency arise. Men will try to power their way out of an emergency."

—Sharon Lee Kegeles, Facilitator of Sport Management, Barry University, Miami Shores, Florida

"Like any good hypochondriac, when I committed to learn how to dive, I first had to make sure that I didn't have some rare disease that could kill me while exploring the depths of the ocean. My $800 electrocardiogram confirmed that I was in good shape and, luckily, my health insurance agreed that I needed this validation. I have run two New York Marathons, hiked Peru's Inca Trail, and generally lived an active lifestyle, and yet I had con-vinced myself that underwater adventure was different, at least much more dangerous since it implicitly requires a life-saving device."

—Amy Richards, New York

to too great a depth and/or ascends too quickly from depths of 60 feet or more. Dive training focuses on techniques and timing that prevent DCS in most cases. In the event that you do suffer from DCI, oxygen, rest, and nonalcoholic beverages combat the condition (see page 83).

- **"Will anything happen to my breast implants?"** The implants themselves won't change, or will do so only minimally, while you're diving. Take special care to ensure your BC fits well and is nonconstricting, because excess tightness across the chest could put pressure on the seams of your implants and cause them to rupture. Saline-filled implants are neutrally buoyant and will not affect

Snorkeling in sheltered waters like the Baths on Virgin Gorda in the Britsh Virgin Islands or shallow dives elsewhere can help take the edge off a new diver's fear of the deep.

your *buoyancy*. However, silicone implants are heavier than water and, especially if they are large, you might need to adjust your weights to compensate.

REALITY CHASES MISPERCEPTIONS

I could probably theorize for pages about why people in general and women in particular harbor many misconceptions about the sea, but there's no point in analyzing why the water holds such a terrifying image for so many people. As Sarah Jane Brown—who with her brother owns a Fort Lauderdale dive business—sees it, easing the transition from fearing to embracing diving is her number-one task.

Brown says that women are wary of the unknown. Many are afraid of jumping off the back of a boat into the water or that fish will touch them.

"We offer free, half-hour scuba lessons right at the resorts," she says. "We get people out of their lounge chairs and let them breathe underwater for half an hour. We mainly deal with people who are on vacation. I say, 'Come and dive with us.' If they spend another two hours in the pool in a resort course, they can dive."

In addition to vacationers who kind of stumble into scuba, Brown notes that "women often get into diving because their husbands or boyfriends do." She also says that "Men will say, 'I'm a diver,' and they talk about it to impress the woman; instead, they scare her. They'll say, 'I went to 120 feet.' They didn't go to 120 feet. They went to 50 feet." For new divers, Brown is an advocate of shore dives, which involve walking in from the beach rather than entering the water from the boat.

Like many other instructors, Brown recognizes the value of diving in shallow waters where the fish are plentiful, which for many people is as good as it gets. She herself learned that way. Born in Great Britain, she moved to Colorado for the mountains and the snow. She went to Lauderdale-by-the-Sea for a vacation one May, dubbed "mud season" in the high country. "I got some gear and paddled out to a reef," she relates. "The water was swirling and there was heavy surge. But I looked through my mask and couldn't believe the beauty in 8 feet of water. I saw how fantastic it was despite the imperfect conditions. I just knew right away that I'd get into the dive business. I moved to Florida, and in two years, I became an instructor."

Chapter 3

🐟 **GEAR TALK**

Humans are not equipped with gills so, at its most basic, dive equipment serves as a life-support system, enabling us to breathe underwater. Any introductory dive session that you sign up for is primarily an equipment orientation; every instruction track, whether resort course or full-certification program, also focuses heavily on equipment.

When you learn the fundamentals of diving, you might feel inundated with the emphasis on gear. Your manual will cover equipment in detail, and so will your instructor. If you watch an instructional videotape, it too will cover the subject. To dive on any level, you need to be comfortable with the gear.

The first pieces of equipment that you probably will buy are a mask, snorkel, and fins, but for convenience, this chapter describes a full set of dive gear from head to toe. See pages 74–76 for a checklist when you decide to gear up.

BORROW, RENT, OR BUY?

When you sign up for your initial introductory session, the dive operator will supply all the gear you need (mask, snorkel, fins, BC, regulator, tank, and weights, all of which are described in this chapter). The dive shop or resort will supply everyone in the group from its inventory, which often means a limited choice (sometimes no choice) of manufacturers and models. There will be a sufficient

MINIMAL MAINTENANCE

Minimal equipment maintenance involves rinsing, or preferably soaking, all your gear in fresh water after each day of diving. Dried salt water can corrode metal parts and stiffen straps and fabrics. Just as you regularly have your car serviced, you should take your regulator and BC to your dive shop once a year to make sure that everything is still sound and functioning. Dive operators are responsible for keeping rental gear in good shape and for annually inspecting all tanks to ensure that they are still safe.

"I've always been interested in equipment and I'm always on the move, so my friends nicknamed me the 'Go-Go, Gear, and Gadget Girl.' I prefer 'Gear and Gadget Girl,' which seems more professional. Others might misconstrue the 'Go-Go' part."

—Patty Newell-Motara, publisher of *Women Underwater Magazine*, Flemington, New Jersey

range of BC and fin sizes to accommodate the group, but don't expect any of it to be especially comfortable. The same holds true when you sign up for lessons; however, by then, you will probably be encouraged to buy at least the mask, snorkel, and fins.

If you dive occasionally, perhaps on vacation, you might not find it worthwhile to invest in dive equipment. If your local dive shop has acceptable gear, you can often rent it to take along. Otherwise, you will rent at your destination. Again, the selection is limited and the fit and comfort are iffy, but it may be economically wise to keep renting. However, if you develop a passion for diving, dive locally, travel often, or simply have a lot of disposable income, you'll soon want your own gear. Whether you choose to borrow, rent, or buy, you will need all the same pieces of equipment to get underwater.

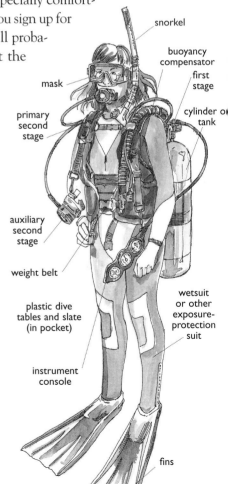

snorkel

buoyancy compensator

first stage

cylinder or tank

mask

primary second stage

auxiliary second stage

weight belt

plastic dive tables and slate (in pocket)

instrument console

wetsuit or other exposure-protection suit

fins

Full diving regalia, from top (mask) to toe (fins).

WOMEN'S EQUIPMENT TEST TEAM

Abundant (some would say excess) information on equipment is found in dive magazines and on the Internet—and most of it is aimed at men. Struck by the inequities of just men evaluating equipment for magazine test reports and the inappropriateness of not much gear designed for women's bodies, dive instructor Jennifer King decided to do something about the situation.

"I started diving in 1980 in cold water and had to tough out equipment issues—wetsuits and BCs that wouldn't fit and all that," she recalls. "When I took my instructor course, I was thrown in with the guys. We took turns being the student and the instructor. They think differently from us."

King began campaigning for women's voices to be heard in the dive industry, and in 1993 she spearheaded the Women's Equipment Test Team (WETT) to evaluate equipment then on the market and to encourage the development of functional gear for women. The dive industry's first response is what WETT calls the SAP Principle—Small and Pink. Companies would take a piece of low-end equipment, make it "small and pink," and call it a woman's model. Thanks to the efforts of King and the WETT, more quality, performance equipment sized for women is now available. "In the mid-1980s, 20 percent of divers were women," King says, "and now it's 40 to 45 percent. We hope that the equipment issue solved some of this."

Although you may be a successful yard-sale shopper or classified-ad cruiser, getting involved with someone else's cast-off dive gear is dicey. If you insist on buying used equipment from a private party, have it inspected, overhauled, and approved by a dive shop. Better yet, buy from the dive shop during an end-of-season sale or purchase its used rental gear that has been well maintained and properly overhauled before it has been put up for sale.

MASK

The mask creates a sealed air space in front of your eyes so that you can focus underwater. It also covers your nostrils so that you can *equalize* the air pressure in your mask and ears as you descend. Swim goggles do allow you to focus underwater, but because they do not cover your nose, they do not allow you to equalize. The technique of equalizing is discussed on page 61.

The dive mask consists of tempered safety-glass lenses—either a pair of lenses like eyeglasses or a single-lens design similar to ski goggles—held by a plastic frame that is surrounded by a skirt of pliable silicone rubber to conform to your face and keep the water out. Some people believe that clearer vision is

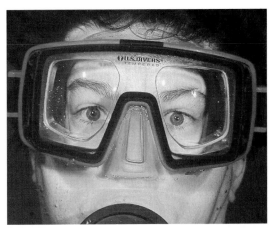

Oh, Red Diving Hood, what big eyes you have! By creating an air space in front of your eyes, the mask enables you to focus underwater. Custom corrective lenses are available if you normally wear glasses or contacts.

Low-Profile Goggles

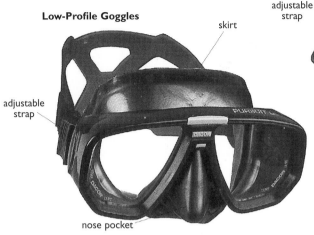

skirt

adjustable strap

adjustable strap

nose pocket

skirt

tempered glass

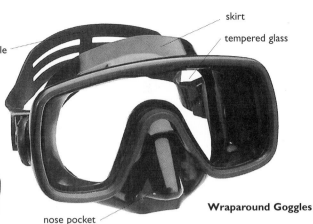

adjustable strap

nose pocket

Wraparound Goggles

You can chose between a **low-profile mask** (left) with twin lenses or a **wraparound mask** (above) with a single lens. The most important feature, however, is a good fit.

"**A** mask is a 'thing' that you put on your face, which means the most important piece of gear goes on the most sensitive part of your body. You have to make sure there are no protrusions or seams in the nose part. If you find a mask that otherwise fits well, you can use Vaseline to protect your nose, or file the protrusion with an emery board. Many women have narrow temples, which some masks don't fit. Masks with clear silicone skirts and extra windows help if you're claustrophobic. The worst feeling is having a mask that leaks during a dive. We've often had to look at problems and adaptations, not problems and solutions."

—Lorraine Bemis-Sadler, equipment director, Women's Scuba Association

provided by a low-profile, wraparound mask, in which the skirt is "short" to bring the lens closer to the eyes.

Quality masks now all feature a double skirt. Think of the inner skirt as the petticoat to help keep water out and enhance comfort, and the outer skirt as—well—the skirt. An adjustable strap keeps the mask on your head. Some straps offer fingertip adjustment so that you can loosen or tighten it easily while you're diving. If you find that the standard silicone mask strap pulls on your hair, you can replace it with one made of cloth or nylon. If you wear your long hair in a ponytail when you dive, look for a split strap.

Skirts are generally clear, but frames come in colors. Frames in a wide range of colors coordinated to your other gear and divewear are available, but make sure that they fit properly and are comfortable.

Fitting a mask

Masks are unisex, but they do come in several sizes to accommodate different head and face sizes. The most important criterion for a mask is that it creates a watertight seal on your face. The simplest way to fit a mask is to loop the strap in front of the mask to keep it out of the way. Then hold the mask comfortably against your face.

Inhale normally through your nose to create suction in the mask. (This technique is nicknamed the "sniff test"—although you aren't trying to smell anything.) If the mask seals against your face and holds there, it fits well. Other experts recommend doing this fit test with a regulator in your mouth. The mask should be comfortable when you're breathing with a regulator. Ideally, the nose pocket will not squeeze or pinch your nose; on a dual-lens model, the mask should not touch the bone above the bridge of your nose.

Mask options and accessories

Single-lens designs offer a greater field of vision, so divers with mild claustrophobia often prefer them. You can also get a dual-lens mask with special features, such as small side lenses for peripheral vision or a top window lens so that you can easily look up (which is actually looking ahead while you're moving underwater). Some masks have a window lens on the bottom so that you can see your buckles and pockets as you access them. Other masks have a *purge valve*—usually located at the nose. This is a one-way valve that allows any seeped-in water to be easily expelled. If this feature appeals to you, make sure that you can still pinch your nose to equalize with the regulator in your mouth, or look for a model with the purge valve on the lower corner of the mask itself.

If you wear eyeglasses, you can order single-vision or bifocal prescription lenses. Fog-free lenses are also available. If seeing natural colors is important, you can investigate color-enhancing or tinted lenses that bring out reds and yellows at depths of 30 feet or more.

Most quality masks come packaged in a rigid plastic case to protect it in your dive bag, while traveling, or when it's stored at home. If your mask doesn't come with a case, you may want to invest in one. Some divers purchase a favorite brand of antifog liquid, but for others, the inelegant act of spitting into the lens works just fine. I Sea U is the name of a rearview mirror that fits on your mask. I haven't tried it, but the company says it's especially comforting to new divers who want to keep their buddies in sight or who worry about a big fish coming up behind them.

Masks start at about $30 ($50 for the self-purge model) for a non-brand-name model from a mail-order catalog, and range as high as about $150 for a top-of-the-line style from a well-known manufacturer. Prescription lenses start at under $100 for single-vision lenses and at about $150 for bifocals. After you buy a mask, you may have to remove a protective coating from the lenses. Non-gel toothpaste and a soft cloth work well for this chore, but make sure you don't scour off the anti-fog coating, if the mask has it. Contact information for mail-order companies is listed in chapter 10, Resources.

SNORKEL

The snorkel, a slightly curved plastic tube with a mouthpiece at one end, is designed so that you can breathe while floating facedown on the water's surface. The basic parts of the snorkel are the tube, the mouthpiece, a clip for affixing it to your mask, and a reservoir at the base of the tube to

• •

"In the past, equipment was a thorn in the side of many women divers. As women became more involved in the sport, manufacturers responded with the SAP Principle. However, offering the same equipment in size small and the color pink did not satisfy the female consumer. Through the efforts of such groups as the WSA, equipment designs were tested and retested. Manufacturers listened, and a handful of BCs designed to fit the female shape have emerged."

—Cynthia Matzke Baer, writing in *Dive Training* magazine

• •

keep residual water out of the airway. The tube usually has one fairly rigid plastic section and one flexible section of silicone rubber for a comfortable fit.

You can draw more air through a large-bore tube, but it's more difficult to expel water from a long one. Therefore, common sense dictates that a relatively short, relatively wide tube would provide the greatest benefits. However, you might be able to find only large-bore tubes with the features you like for diving. Short ones are usually designed for children, not adult divers, and are sold with sporting goods for kids. Snorkels are available in several colors that can be coordinated with the rest of your gear.

Snorkels are used for more than just surface swimming. You will use yours to skin dive, after you surface from a dive, or to conserve air while you're waiting on the surface for your group to assemble for a dive in choppy seas. When water splashes in, you need to expel it with a sharp exhale. Because snorkels are open on top, water can still enter the tube, which is the reason for the small reservoir below the mouthpiece. This helps prevent taking in water along with air as you inhale. Some models are self-draining to keep them relatively water-free. A few also feature a one-way purge valve to expel water or a splash guard to minimize splash-in. At least one company makes a "dry snorkel" with a ball that floats inside the tube to prevent water from entering. The clip, which is usually about halfway up the tube, is used to attach the snorkel to your mask strap. Because their air hoses come over the right shoulder, divers customarily attach snorkels to the left side of their masks. Snorkels range from $15 to $50.

large bore

designed with smooth bends

flexible tube no longer than 17 in.

mouthpiece

clip

A **snorkel** is a simple device that you'll use often, for snorkeling, skin diving, or to conserve air while floating on the surface before or after a dive.

self-draining barrel

BUOYANCY COMPENSATOR

The "vest" that divers wear goes by several names. Officially, it's called a *buoyancy compensator* (BC) or *buoyancy control device* (BCD). You can call it whatever you want, but you can't dive without it. When the airtight bladder lining is inflated, you can float on the surface—even with a heavy air tank on your back and weights around your middle. To submerge, you must let the air out of your BC. When you're diving and breathing off your tank, which lightens it, you must let a little air at a time into the BC so that you remain neutrally buoyant. (This is explained in detail on pages 49–50.)

The BC has functional parts and convenience features. All models have an *inflator hose*, permanently attached to the vest's left shoulder with a coupling, via one of the regulator hoses, to the tank. This hose has two buttons—one to release air from the BC and one to inflate it. It also has a mouthpiece so you can blow into it to inflate it if necessary. Most BCs also feature a *dump valve* (found in the rear upper shoulder or lower corner of the bladder), which enables you to release all the air from the bladder with one quick pull. To dump air from the BC, you pull on a small ball attached to a string. Many models also feature quick-release buckles on the shoulder straps that make it easier to get in to or out of the BC.

quick-release shoulder strap

carrying handle

hose retainer

inflator hose

mouthpiece

power inflator

dump valve

dump valve

cummerbund

waist strap

The **buoyancy compensator** (BC) is a critical piece of equipment both to keep you afloat on the surface before and after you dive, and to enable you to remain neutrally buoyant underwater.

On the back of the BC is a rigid support against which the tank is mounted with heavy-duty straps of nylon webbing and positive-locking buckles to secure the tank to the BC. A cummerbund-width inner belt, with a Velcro or buckle closure attached to the inside of the BC keeps it from riding up; on many models, a sternum strap snugs it to your body. Other common features include a veritable symphony of pockets, D-rings, and hose retainers so that you can carry a slate, a *dive light* for night diving, a waterproof fish-identification chart, *dive tables*, and other gizmos and gadgets, or so that you can batten down extra hoses. (The following description of the regulator describes these hoses.) Some BCs also incorporate special pockets to hold dive weights, eliminating the need for a separate weight belt; this is referred to as an *integrated weight design*.

Women's models

For years, all BCs were unisex-sized, and women had to do their best to find a model within the range of sizes from men's small to extra large. Now, numerous manufacturers offer at least one model sized and shaped for women. The most obvious accommodation for women is our different body shape, including breasts, which unisex BCs tend to squeeze down. Some of the ways designers have adjusted for women include cuts that fit the BC around, not over, the chest and bladders that only inflate outward. At least one manufacturer offers an optional "chest enclosure," designed for warmth without constriction.

Women tend to have shorter torsos than men, another reason standard BCs just don't fit many of us well. They may ride up in back and under the arms, causing discomfort and straining the back and shoulders. On women's models, shoulder straps are contoured or modified with a narrower width for slimmer shoulders and have additional foam padding. Other features that address fit and comfort problems include integrated weight systems, adjustable torso lengths, and padded backpacks to distribute tank weight. The size range has also been adjusted, from women's extra small to large. Keep in mind that, especially for nontropical diving, integrated weights can make a rig too heavy to handle out of the water.

It pays to shop around and try on several BCs when you're ready to buy, for this is a big-ticket investment that can last for years. Proper fit is the most important consideration, so be sure to try on a BC over the thickness of the wetsuit or *dive skin* that you plan to wear most of the time, and inflate it to make sure that you can breathe fully. I've had a few bad diving experiences, and every one involved ill-fitting, unisex rental gear, particularly straight-cut BCs that squeezed my ribcage so that I couldn't inhale a lungful of air. Also, if you're short, as I am, make sure that your inflator hose isn't longer than your arm, because you must extend it fully over your head to submerge. One option is a model with an air dump for descents. For a list of companies that make BCs for women, see page 135.

While many women prefer women's model BCs, others are comfortable in unisex models that often come with a wider range of features and at more price points. Another potential problem with women's models impacts divers in temperate or colder waters: because they are smaller, women's BCs don't always have the lift required for the increased weight a diver carries to accommodate a thicker wetsuit or *dry suit*.

REBREATHERS

In an equipment-heavy sport like scuba diving, aficionados often talking about the latest, greatest, sexiest piece of equipment. For instance, you will often hear divers talking about *rebreathers*, touted as an efficient new development in breathing apparatus. Rebreathers use residual oxygen that is expelled with each breath and at the same time they remove carbon dioxide. They're designed to be silent and virtually bubblefree. In contrast to a conventional scuba setup, which is referred to as an *open-circuit system* because all exhaled air is expelled through the regulator, rebreathers are of two types. The semiclosed circuit expels a portion of exhaled gases, and the fully closed circuit recirculates all of the air during the dive. The stored air is then expelled during the ascent. Rebreathers were first developed for military use with the goal of divers avoiding detection. Marine biologists and underwater photographers and videographers were next to appreciate silent, nearly bubblefree diving, and eventually, rebreathers began catching on with the technology-oriented—and well-heeled—segment of the recreational dive community. Rebreathers use enriched air (see page 85) and require special training. As a beginning diver, you probably won't hop right out and buy such a rig. Rebreathers cost $3,000 to $15,000.

BCs vary widely in price, from the mid-$300s to $700 or more. A good-quality BC for tropical diving will set you back $450 to $500, but if you plan to do temperate or cold-water diving in places such as the Great Lakes, Puget Sound, the Atlantic Coast from the Carolinas on north, or along the California coast, you need a BC that will enable you to stay neutrally buoyant when you're weighted for a thick wetsuit or drysuit. Therefore, make sure your BC provides sufficient lift for the most demanding conditions in which you plan to dive, which might raise the price.

A **dry suit**, which makes cold-water diving possible in such places as Washington State's Puget Sound, requires additional weights and a BC capable of lifting that extra weight. Many divers need some help in adjusting all of this gear.

REGULATOR

The regulator with its allied devices, all connected via hoses that resemble an octopus or a spider, is command central for your diving. This device enables you to breathe and to fill your BC by converting the high-pressure air in your tank to *ambient pressure*—the lower, usable pressure that equals the water pressure at whatever depth you're diving. The single word *regulator* is a catchall for several devices that are all interconnected via hoses: the *first stage, second stage, mouthpiece, octopus,* and *instrument console.* Its functions include monitoring water pressure and delivering breathable air at the same pressure as the water surrounding you at any dive depth.

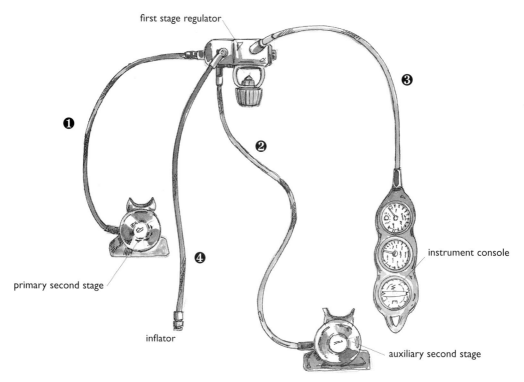

first stage regulator

❶

❷

❸

instrument console

primary second stage

❹

inflator

auxiliary second stage

The **octopus** is a complicated beast. Here's its anatomy: first-stage regulator; primary second stage with hose (**1**); auxiliary second stage with hose (**2**); instrument console with hose (**3**); inflator device that attaches to the BC with hose (**4**).

The *first-stage regulator* resembles a chrome cylinder with a big knurled knob on it, or a barrel with protruding screw threads. It attaches directly to the top of the compressed-air tank. Its purpose is to begin adjusting the compressed air from the tank and dispersing it to the second stage, octopus, and instrument gauges. The first stage does all this via four hoses. One hose (1) connects the first stage and *primary second stage*. Another hose (2) connects the first stage and the *auxiliary* or *emergency second stage*. A third hose (3) leads to the *instrument console*, which monitors the air supply in your tank, among other functions. A fourth hose (4) is used to inflate the *BC*.

The two hoses, (1) and (2), connecting the first stage to the primary second stage and the auxiliary second stage are the parts of the regulator from which you breathe. Via a mouthpiece on the second stage, air pressure is further reduced to the ambient pressure necessary for breathing comfortably underwater. Although regulators are gender-neutral, many women prefer models with more compact second stages, which are smaller and lighter in weight and, therefore, reduce jaw fatigue. Women with smaller mouths may also find standard mouthpieces uncomfortable. If that is your situation, investigate after-market or even custom models.

Inside the second stage is the *inlet valve*, which permits one-way air flow—from the tank to you. This is an on-demand rather than a constant air flow, which means that when you inhale, air moves from the tank through the regulator to your body. A second one-way valve, called the *exhaust valve*, permits exhaled air to escape, causing bubbles to rise to the surface. If you manually need to expel air

The most basic instrument gauge is a **console** with analog displays to monitor depth and air remaining in the tank.

and water from the regulator, you can push the purge valve on the second stage. The auxiliary second stage, also called the *alternate air source* or octopus, enables you to share your air with another diver in an emergency.

The third hose (3) leads to your submersible instrument console, which contains a pressure gauge to show your tank's air pressure measured in psi (pounds per square inch) and a depth gauge that shows your dive depth measured in feet. And the last hose (4) comes from the first stage and attaches to your BC, allowing you to inflate the bladder. Traditional analog gauges have dials that display air pressure, dive depth, and often compass direction, too. Analog consoles on regulators are being phased out. Newer electronic instruments, called *dive computers*, provide the same information—and much more—on digital displays, and some even newer hoseless models have sensors mounted directly on the first stage that send data to a wrist-mounted computer. Dive computers are gaining in popularity. Some divers like to be technically current, but computers are more than just a jazzy status symbol. They have the practical benefit of being able to read and store a great deal of information in order to create a *dive profile*—how long you dived, what your maximum depth was, how much air you consumed, and more. Before you submerge, you will have a *dive plan* (see page 52). The profile is what you actually do.

Expect to pay $200 to $1,600 for a regulator. The lower price range includes functional models; the higher end includes titanium models with the knobs and switches that experienced divers might have to use to regulate air supply under highly technical diving conditions. Dive computers range from $250 to $1,300. The less expensive models are just as reliable as the costlier ones; they simply process less data and, therefore, display fewer minutiae about your dive.

BUILT-IN SAFETY

When a new diver considers the life-support system consisting of the tank, regulator, and hoses designed for breathing underwater, it seems as if there are numerous things that can go wrong. In fact, the system is not only time-tested and reliable, but it's also designed to supply more air than you actually need. You also have a spare regulator mouthpiece (auxiliary second stage) that you could switch to in case of mechanical problems with your primary regulator, and you have a dive buddy who can share air with you via his or her auxiliary second stage. Many beginners dive in a guided group, with a divemaster or instructor nearby. In case of an emergency, remember that two people can breathe off one tank while ascending safely to the surface. Also, many experienced divers now carry a small tank with its own regulator, called a *pony bottle* or *Spare Air*.

With a compressed-air tank on her back and a regulator in her mouth, this diver is able to breathe underwater.

TANK

The official name for the device that contains compressed air is *cylinder*, but most people refer to it as a *tank*. But if you want to sound savvy, what you really need to remember is that this piece of equipment is not an oxygen tank, because beginning recreational divers do not breathe pure oxygen any more than landlubbers do. Dive cylinders are made of steel or aluminum. Your first-stage regulator is connected to an on-off valve at the top. Cylinders come in various sizes. If you become a passionate diver and dive in local waters, you may eventually buy your own. If you fly to dive, you most likely will never buy your own. However, in the beginning, you'll use what the dive operator offers—generally an Aluminum-80, which holds 80 cubic feet of compressed air.

As you become more comfortable in the water, use air efficiently, and—if you're diving in warm water—use less weight, you may find that a 65-cubic-foot tank suffices. Not only does it weigh less, but it also is about 6 inches shorter, which makes it more comfortable on your back, especially if you're short-waisted.

WEIGHTS

To counteract your body's natural buoyancy and the buoyancy created by air spaces in your gear, you need to wear lead weights. The amount depends on such factors as your body weight, the kind of *exposure suit* you're wearing, whether you're diving in salt water or freshwater, and your skill as a diver.

The basic weight system is a belt made of nylon webbing on which you thread the weights. The most common weights are squares or rectangles with slots for the belt. The weight belt is generally worn below the BC and on the hips, which some women find uncomfortable. To relieve this discomfort, options include weight belts with padded pockets, integrated-weight BCs with built-in pockets to hold weights, ankle weights, and soft weights, which are made of pellet-like shot in soft pouches that conform to your body's curves.

Some people refer to the modern way of weighting as "weight distribution system," which describes the trend to moving weights off the belt and onto other parts of the body. "I feel the weight distribution system is particularly appropriate for women, because many women need more weight than do men of similar size," says Women's Scuba Association equipment director Lorraine Bemis-Sadler. "Weights may be put into BC pockets, other places on the body, or even

• •

"**W**hen buying fins, a small woman may want a
 shorter blade. Driving a fin that is too big through
 the water is exhausting."

—Lorraine Bemis-Sadler, equipment director, Women's Scuba Association

• •

Full-foot fins are suitable for snorkeling
and warm-water diving, but **adjustable
fins**, worn with **booties**, are needed in
cold water and for shore dives where
you walk into the water, often over rock.

**Adjustable
(open-heel) Fin**

Full-Foot Fin

on the tank. Ankle weights may help buoyancy problems from
floating legs by keeping the legs at a better angle for swimming, and help the whole body stay at a more comfortable position in the water."

Dive operators at resort destinations generally
include both the tank and weights in the cost of a dive
trip, because both are heavy and awkward to travel
with; however, if you want your own, you'll find
them to be the least expensive component of your
dive gear.

FINS

Just as nondivers mistakenly refer to dive
cylinders as *oxygen tanks*, they call fins *flippers*,
which is descriptive but not cool. When you dive,
you not only will refer to this basic equipment by the
correct name, but you will also have to make a decision as to
which of two basic types is best for you. Whichever type you
select, a larger or stiffer blade provides more propulsion power but
requires more strength.

With a full-foot fin, you slip your entire bare foot into a foot pocket.
This type of fin is most suitable for snorkeling and warm-water diving when you walk in from a
sandy beach. If you buy a pair, select the appropriate size so that your foot neither falls out nor is
constricted.

Adjustable fins have foot pockets into which you slip just your forefoot and adjustable heel
straps to affix the fins to your feet. They are worn with ankle-high, neoprene dive booties with
rubber soles. Even though wearing adjustable fins is more expensive, scuba divers tend to prefer
this style, because the booties provide additional warmth and the rubber soles are good to wear
on a boat's slippery deck or when crossing a pebbly or hot sand beach on a shore dive. Think of
full-foot fins as resembling pumps and adjustable fins as resembling sling-back shoes. Fins range
in price from about $50 to $175, and booties cost $30 to $100.

THE GLOVE GAME

• • • • • • • • • • • • • • • • • • • •

If you dive in cold water, dive gloves are mandatory for warmth. In tropical waters, they are more of a wise option. They protect your hands from abrasion, should you inadvertently touch coral or rock, or irritation from a stinging critter that comes in contact with your skin. However, wearing gloves is not a license to touch living things intentionally. "If you have gloves on, you're more tempted to touch the coral," acknowledges Ellen Horne of the Coral Reef Alliance, "and although touching fish and other marine animals is not recommended, it's less harmful to touch fish with gloves than without."

Touching underwater plants and animals is not recommended, for both the critter's well-being and the diver's. If you feel you *must* touch something, do so very gently and only with gloves on, as this diver is doing with a pufferfish.

The newest concept is *split-fin* designs that work on a propulsion principle, rather than on the traditional paddle principle, to help the diver move through the water. With conventional blades, the length and size of the blade determine its power, and some women have trouble handling a large blade. The split-fin blade, inspired by a fish's tail, relies on the shape for efficiency. To visualize the principle, think of a paddle-wheel boat, which operates less efficiently than a propeller-driven boat, even though the propeller is physically smaller than a paddle-wheel.

EXPOSURE PROTECTION

In the movies, the voluptuous female diver embarks on all her underwater adventures in a T-shirt that clings provocatively to her bikini-clad body. In reality, divers cover up more underwater. Even in tropical waters, where *hypothermia* is less of an issue, wearing something under the BC prevents chafing and irritation, and also offers *exposure protection* from abrasion and contact with little undersea critters that might cause a rash or an itch.

When you're underwater, you will therefore wear some kind of an *exposure suit*. In warm water, many divers like the comfort of a dive skin, a one-piece Lycra bodysuit that provides abrasion protection but insulates minimally. Dive skins are economical, comfortable, and flattering. If you need a little insulation, consider combining a dive skin and a neoprene vest. Many wetsuits come in alleged unisex cuts, but women's models are also widely available. Women who dive a lot frequently have a suit custom-made for them.

Wetsuits, available in various cuts and thicknesses to conserve body heat in different water temperatures, are suitable for tropical to temperate waters. These one- or two-piece, zip-up neoprene exposure suits are sometimes lined with Polartec fleece. The neoprene itself insulates your skin from direct contact with the water, and your body warms your perspiration and any water that seeps into the suit.

Wetsuit styles include the *full suit* (long legs, long sleeves), the *shortie* (short legs and long or short sleeves), and the two-piece suit (*Farmer John* or *Farmer Jane*, high-waisted overalls and a separate jacket). You can wear a thin suit in warm water. If you're diving in colder water, you will obviously want to get a suit of suitable thickness for the water temperature. Some cold-water divers wear a wetsuit jacket or at least a vest over a thick one-piece wetsuit. Another option is what manufacturers describe as a *semi-dry suit*, which is a wetsuit designed to reduce the effect of sea water entering and flushing out of the suit, draining your body heat with it.

Or, for really cold water, you may need an inflatable *dry suit*, which is waterproof with watertight openings at the neck, wrists, and ankles. A dry suit is worn over thermal garments, which—along with the dry trapped air—keep you warm. Make sure that wrists, ankles, neck, and zipper are tight but not constricting. If you tend to get cold or dive in nontropical waters, a *dive hood* is also a good idea. Because heat loss through the head is significant, wearing a dive hood might enable you to get away with a thinner wetsuit—and, therefore, less *lead* on your weight belt.

Wetsuit prices vary widely. You can find an off-brand mail-order or discount-store wetsuit for under $100, but the cut won't

EXPOSURE PROTECTION TIPS

• • • • • • • • • • • • • • •

The following chart provides general guidelines for recommended wetsuit thickness. Note that there is considerable overlap in temperature ranges to accommodate individual tastes and body thermostats. Keep in mind, however, that women, thin people, and older people tend to lose body heat and get chilled sooner than others.

EXPOSURE SUITS

Water Temperature	Recommended Thickness
75–85 degrees	$\frac{1}{16}$ inch (1.6 mm) neoprene, Lycra, or Polartec dive skins
70–85 degrees	$\frac{1}{8}$ inch (3 mm) neoprene
65–75 degrees	$\frac{3}{16}$ inch (5 mm) neoprene
50–70 degrees	$\frac{1}{4}$ inch (6.5 mm) neoprene
35–65 degrees	$\frac{3}{8}$ inch (9.5 mm) neoprene, or dry suit at lower ranges

A **shortie wetsuit** suffices for tropical diving.

be great, the neoprene will be low-grade, and it probably won't hold up for very long. A semi-dry suit or full-on dry suit will cost $500 or more, and few are made in women-specific sizes (although some do come in a short length). The price is high, but if you're a cold-water diver, you can't do without one.

Other divewear accessories include gloves for exposure and abrasion protection, and hoods, which are mandatory for cold-water diving. Some women with long hair like to wear a light hood, even in warm water, because it keeps their hair from tangling on itself or with the mask strap.

Chapter 4

READY, SET, LEARN TO DIVE

Just as a solid building is erected on a firm foundation, solid diving is built on an understanding of its principles and on practicing the skills it takes to put the theories to work. Your instructor may talk about the three P's of diving: preparation, prevention, and performance. *Preparation* means getting yourself mentally and physically ready to dive, and readying your equipment as well. *Prevention* means training in the skills you need to prevent problems from occurring in the first place and keeping small problems from turning into major accidents. *Performance* means taking your training seriously and implementing your knowledge when you dive. This chapter provides a preview of what you can expect in class and how you can make physical preparations for diving. Perhaps you already have.

TUNE YOUR BODY FOR DIVING

The issue of fitness in diving parallels fitness in other sports—or in life in general. Diving, like any other physical activity, is easier and more pleasurable if you're reasonably fit. Once you start diving, you may be surprised to find a greater proportion of overweight aficionados than in most sports. You'll even find chunky instructors and divemasters, and you might decide that if they can carry extra poundage, so can you. After all, you can always compensate for extra body fat with additional weights, right? The fact that you *can* compensate for *avoirdupois* doesn't mean that you *should*.

There are no exercises that are specific to scuba diving. In the long run, you will be a better diver if you're generally fit. Instructors, divemasters, dive guides, and boat crews help with the equipment, but for many women, part of diving is having the strength to handle their own gear with minimal assistance. If your muscle tone is missing, now is the time to begin strength training. You can join a gym or work out at home to shape up. Your best bet is to find a good program with free weights or machines for general body strengthening and toning. If you can find a personal trainer who happens to be a scuba diver, so much the better. But whether you work with a trainer or go it alone, your weight-training program should include both upper-body conditioning (i.e., shoulders, chest, arms, and back) and lower-body work (i.e., abdominals, legs, and gluteals) to ensure that you feel stronger when you begin to dive. Remember to warm up before each workout and to cool down and stretch afterwards.

Your energy expenditure while diving is less than a day of cross-country skiing or training for a marathon, but more than a sprinter or a pole-vaulter. You're highly unlikely to spend more than an hour at a time underwater, but diving still requires a degree of stamina. At the very least, you must be able to swim underwater, perhaps against the current and climb up the ladder of a dive boat. Sometimes you will need to struggle against ocean surge. When you do a shore dive, you have to be able to walk from the beach in full regalia until the water is deep enough to paddle or float—and then out onto the beach again when you're finished diving.

WHERE TO START

Remember that you can get certified where you live, on vacation, or a combination of the two. There are nearly 2,000 dive training centers in the United States, but don't let this overwhelm

These new divers are practicing setting up their equipment on a sunny dock in Belize.

you. When it comes to selecting one, geography is destiny. If you learn to dive where you live, the options are limited to nearby facilities. Local learn-to-dive programs are operated by dive shops that also sell and rent diving equipment, organize dive trips, and may have an on-site travel agency. Because these businesses want to build and maintain a hometown client base, they are experts at running classroom instruction and pool sessions—and they take beginner classes to a nearby site for open-water checkout dives.

You can also undertake the entire certification process while on vacation.

"I did all my course work with our local dive shop and scheduled one of their dive trips to Cayman Brac where I did my check-out dives for certification. I felt better going with the folks who trained me than going with strangers, especially since I was 'buddyless' (my husband won't dive). I dived all week with one of the instructors from our dive shop, and she and I had a great time. I even did a night dive with her—the octopi were great."

—Barb Seamon, Strongsville, Ohio

SPECIALIZED SCUBA CENTERS

Elsewhere, some local dive shops have their own in-store training pools or even small dive ponds in the backyard. But Texas does everything bigger. The Reef, located in Houston, just a 10-minute drive from the Astrodome, features a 20-acre spring-fed lake. Its average depth is 40 feet, and it boasts six docks, four underwater training platforms, and wreck dives on 24 sunken boats and three school buses. The lake is aquifer-fed, resulting in visibility of a respectable 15 feet. With a dive school, it's a great place to learn, and with a tank-filling station, it's also excellent for learning to dive independently in a somewhat controlled setting. Not even the Spanish Main boasts more wrecks in a smaller area than The Reef. Divers dive, and nondivers can enjoy swimming, paddle sports, and fishing.

If you decide on your destination first, geography again limits the options. Dive operators at tropical resort destinations offer the same programs as at-home dive shops—in other words, retail sales, rentals, and instruction—according to the standards of an international certifying agency. In addition, they have specially equipped boats to take divers to dive spots, and they can fill air tanks and service scuba gear for more experienced independent divers. These operators may be located in town, along a strip of beachfront stores, or on-site at a resort hotel.

To combine the two ways to get certified, start at home with the theory and the confined-water classes, and then finish with your open-water certification dives while on vacation. This may be on a trip organized by your local dive shop or at a resort dive center under the aegis of the same certifying agency as your dive shop at home. In fact, your local shop can probably refer you to one at your dive destination.

Wherever you learn to dive, the ideal program has small classes (preferably six students per instructor, but no more than eight). Ideally, too, your instructor isn't a newbie, but rather is experienced at teaching diving fundamentals. Patience, good people skills, and a hefty degree of empathy for those who are fearful are all pluses. It's also helpful if the instructor has an assistant to help students with problems, both theoretical and

● ●

"**W**omen often feel forced into the sport and don't like it. They're not doing it because they're interested, but doing it for someone else. The majority I see are dependent on their male companions. I try to get women to take a one-hour Women in Diving course to show them how to begin relying on themselves. I tell them, 'Use your head and know your limits.' "

—Sharon Greer, instructor, Merritt Island, Florida

● ●

especially in the pool. Some people do fine going through the entire process in a concentrated weekend program, but many others do better when the classroom portion is spread out over several consecutive weeks. You know your own learning style, so only you can judge what's right for you.

Women's classes

In a typical coed dive class, the instructor should be sensitive to the differences in men's and women's learning styles, as well as to the dynamics of some couples who try to learn a sport together. Too often that doesn't happen, and the woman is usually the loser. In many cases, a woman tends to defer to her partner's strength or knowledge—real or perceived—and doesn't reach her own potential.

Some dive operators address the issue by occasionally offering courses for women only, with female instructors, assistants, and students; more would do so if a real demand developed. Women have a different style of learning a new physical activity that is often more cerebral and analytical than men, who sometimes think they can muscle through any new situation. Women also react differently to fear: they express their concerns verbally rather than hide them. Women respond favorably to support and encouragement, rather than daring and belittling, in overcoming fear. Women-only classes are so successful in introducing women to the sport that dive shops who offer them occasionally organize trips just for women. I even found a dive boat in the Bahamas with an all-woman crew, including the captain.

● ●

"**O**ur goal is to turn women into independent divers. Many times, if we have couples in class, we break them up. Women tend to blossom after a women-only dive trip. It's gratifying to see them before and after. We had one client that we just couldn't get certified locally. 'I'll get my certification in Cozumel,' she said. And she did."

—Joyce "J.J." Wiebbecke, House of Pelican, Arvada, Colorado

● ●

WHAT TO EXPECT

Here's the scenario: You sampled scuba diving in the nurturing environment of a pool and decided that you want to get certified. You signed up for the class at the dive center and you bought your mask, snorkel, and fins. You have the class schedule and you marked the time and date on your calendar. Now what?

School days

Unless you decide to buy a video and embark on independent study for this part of your dive training, you will learn the theory of diving in a classroom. First, your instruc-

Classroom learning includes hands-on instruction and emphasizes the principles and theory of diving, followed by practice in the pool.

tor introduces him- or herself and you meet your classmates with whom you will share this new adventure. The instructor explains each section of the course, perhaps shows videos, and answers questions. Collateral material includes a textbook or course book of some kind, worksheets and a series of written quizzes, and/or a written final test. The subjects comprise the foundation of theory on which diving practices are built. Some become clear immediately, others make more sense when you apply them in the pool. Here is a sampling of the key topics that your course will cover—in depth, of course.

- **Equipment.** The introduction to scuba gear in chapter 3 outlines the function and importance of each piece of equipment. If you participated in an introductory in-water session before you signed up for a learn-to-dive program, you actually got in some equipment practice before learning the principles.

- **Buoyancy.** Controlling buoyancy is one of the linchpins of safe and responsible scuba diving. To submerge, dive in control, and ascend safely at the end of a dive, you need to manage your buoyancy. You will practice this frequently in the pool, but understanding it helps you accomplish it when you get into the water. Buoyancy is a balancing act that you and your equipment perform so you can dive near a sea or lake bottom without either sinking or popping up like a cork.

    There are three levels of buoyancy: positive (floating), negative (sinking), and neutral (like Baby Bear's porridge, this is "just right" because it's stable—neither sinking nor floating). Neutral buoyancy is to the underwater environment what weightlessness is to outer space. Buoyancy control is a combination of weight (what your body and dive gear weigh); volume (the amount of water you and your gear displace); and air trapped in your body, dive equipment, and clothing. Body size, weight, and percentage of body fat affect your buoyancy. The thickness and material of your exposure suit affect your buoyancy. So does your tank, which displaces a certain amount of water. In addition to the physical volume of your body and your tank, buoyancy is affected by air in your BC or hoses and how much compressed air is contained in your cylinder. Every breath affects your buoyancy. You rise slightly with every inhalation and sink slightly with every exhalation. Throughout the dive, you learn to adjust the air in your BC and control your breathing to remain neutrally buoyant.

An object that floats is **positively buoyant**, one that sinks is **negatively buoyant**, and one that neither sinks not floats is **neutrally buoyant**. This principle holds true even when the "object" is a diver. A properly weighted, neutrally buoyant diver will float on the surface at goggle level. Inhaling causes her to rise slightly **(A)**; exhaling results in slight sinking **(B)**.

●   **Air and Hydrostatic (or Water) Pressure.** Both physics and physiology are involved when it comes to pressure and diving. Anything that is submerged in water is compressed and anything that rises in water expands—including the human body. The formulas developed for safe diving take into account these principles of air pressure and *hydrostatic pressure* and their effect on the human body.

Air pressure at sea level is referred to as "one atmosphere," abbreviated as "1 ATA." At 10 meters below the surface (approximately 33 feet), sea-water pressure is twice the air pressure than at sea level, which is abbreviated as 2 ATA. Each additional 10 meters exerts one additional atmosphere of pressure; therefore, the deeper you go, the more pressure the water exerts. (The numbers are somewhat different for fresh-water and high-altitude diving, such as in a mountain lake.)

Furthermore, air volume compresses underwater and air density increases, in direct relation to the depth (as shown in the following table). Your instructor may ask you to visualize a plastic bottle or a balloon, which collapses when it is taken underwater and compressed by the water because the air volume decreases. As you descend, the same thing happens to your body. Increasing water pressure begins to squeeze in your ears and sinuses, and presses your mask against your face. Your regulator is designed to adjust the pressure in your lungs, but it can only do this while you're breathing steadily. When you understand these principles, you know why you must equalize the pressure as you descend, continue breathing steadily throughout the dive to protect your lungs, and how to ascend safely so that your body can readjust to decreasing water pressure.

● ●

Water Pressure

Depth	Pressure	Air Volume	Air Density
Surface 0 meters/0 feet	1 ATA	1	X1
10 meters/33 feet	2 ATA	$\frac{1}{2}$	X2
20 meters/66 feet	3 ATA	$\frac{1}{3}$	X3
30 meters/99 feet	4 ATA	$\frac{1}{4}$	X4
40 meters/132 feet	5 ATA	$\frac{1}{5}$	X5

● ●

●   **Nitrogen Absorption.** The air we breathe is 78 percent nitrogen, 20 percent oxygen, and 2 percent other gases. As you descend during a dive, the amount of air dissolved in your body increases. Your body uses the oxygen and would normally dispel the excess nitrogen, but it cannot do so underwater because of the hydrostatic pressure. While you're underwater, this nitrogen accumulates in your bloodstream and tissues, where it forms small bubbles. If you ascend too quickly, or if you dive again too soon, these bubbles will fizz, much like a carbonated beverage when the container is opened. At the least, you will be uncomfortable; at the worst, you can get severe DCS, more commonly known as *the bends*, which must be treated medically. In *no-decompression diving*, your dive plan will include a three-minute *safety stop* at 15 feet to begin expelling the nitrogen bubbles. (For more information on DCS, see page 83.)

- **Dive Planning.** Simply stated, a *dive plan* involves maximum depth, *bottom time*, and details of the dive you will make. Your dive plan must be based on the length of time that you can safely stay underwater, which is in inverse proportion to the depth of your dive. Therefore, you can make a relatively short, relatively deep dive, or a relatively long, relatively shallow one, or a comparable medium-deep, medium-length dive. To help plan your day, each dive is converted into what is known as a *pressure group*, which is a formula combining your dive's depth and duration. In addition, you must plan on staying on the surface for a specified minimum length of time after each dive, called the *surface interval*, which is based on the pressure group and how many dives you have done. The reason for all these requirements is physiological. Remember, as you breathe compressed air, you use the oxygen while the residual nitrogen lingers in your bloodstream. Your body needs time to process it out, as discussed previously.

    The traditional way of calculating this information is by using *dive tables*, which are charts that determine the progression of a day's diving. In reality, when you go on a guided trip on a commercial dive boat—which is common for new divers—the instructor or divemaster will tell you what your dive plan should be. "Our first dive will be to 80 feet for 30 minutes, with a three-minute safety stop at 15 feet" is an example of information included in a pre-dive briefing. Most advanced divers (and even some novices) now dive with computers that calculate all the numbers and formulas. However, think of working the dive tables as a necessary tool, much like learning how to drive a stick shift or change a tire. You may never *need* it, but knowing how to use dive tables is a good skill to possess.

- **Aquatic Environment.** You will learn about the vagaries of the sea (e.g., waves, surf, surge, and undertow). You won't put this knowledge into practice in the pool, but it comes in handy once you're certified and out there in the open water. You will also learn about the underwater environment and how not to harm it. (See chapter 8.)

UNDERWATER LANGUAGE

You can splurge on high-tech underwater communications devices that actually permit you to talk and listen to other divers underwater, or you can use the more common low-tech dive slates on which you can write underwater. There is even an organization called Sea Signs (see chapter 10, Resources), which promotes the use of sign language by divers. But the lingua franca of the undersea world is still the hand signal, especially for common situations. Unless indicated otherwise, keep your hand in front of your body when signaling. Here are the signals that you and your instructor are most likely to use.

1. **OK.** Raise your right hand to shoulder height. Then, with an open palm, make a circle with your thumb and forefinger. If you're wearing thick gloves, make a fist.

2. **Going Down.** Raise your right hand to shoulder height. Make a fist and extend your thumb downward.

3. **Going Up.** Raise your right hand to shoulder height, with palm toward your body. Make a fist and extend your thumb upward.

4. **Can't Clear Ears.** Point to your ear with one forefinger.

5. **Level Off at This Depth.** Raise your right hand to chest level, palm down and fingers extended.

6. **Go That Way.** Raise one hand to shoulder height, with palm toward your body. Make a fist and extend your forefinger in the direction that you wish your buddy to go.

(continued on next page)

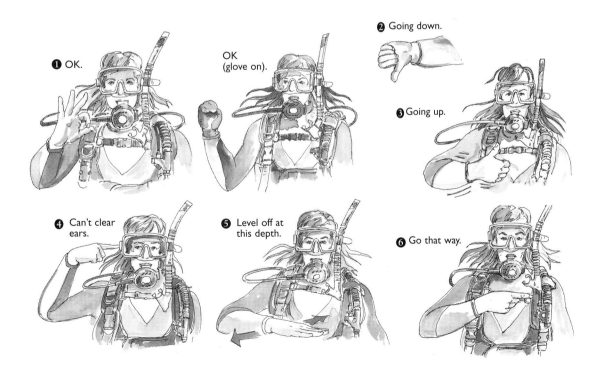

❶ OK.

OK (glove on).

❷ Going down.

❸ Going up.

❹ Can't clear ears.

❺ Level off at this depth.

❻ Go that way.

UNDERWATER LANGUAGE

• •

(continued from previous page)

7.   **Which Way?** If you do not understand the Go That Way signal, raise one hand to shoulder height, make a fist, extend your thumb, and swivel your hand back and forth to indicate your confusion about the intended direction.

8.   **Watch Me.** Point to your chest. This is a signal that your instructor uses often when demonstrating a skill.

9.   **Look at That.** (not pictured) Point to your goggles with your index and middle fingers, and then to the object to which you want to draw attention.

10.   **Something Is Wrong.** Raise your right hand to shoulder height, with palm down. Splay your fingers wide and move your hand up and down.

11.   **Danger!** Raise your arm straight out, to the side, to or just above shoulder level, and make a fist—as if ready to pound on an invisible table.

12.   **Get Closer to Your Buddy.** Make fists with both of your hands, extend your forefingers, and bring them next to each other in front of your chest.

13.   **Low on Air.** Bring your right hand close beside your regulator and point to it.

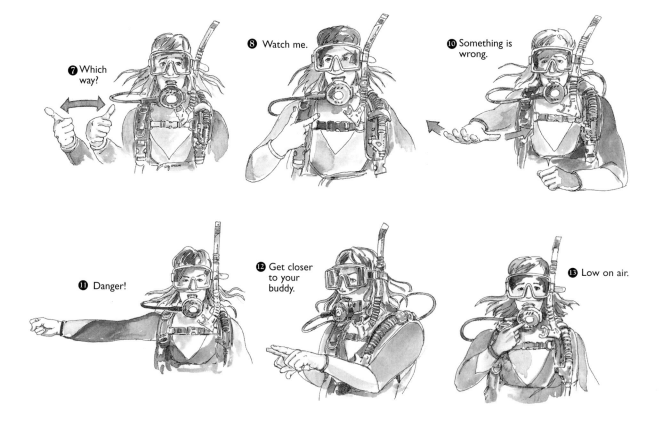

UNDERWATER LANGUAGE

• •

14. **Out of Air.** Bring your right hand to your throat and make a "throat-cutting" motion.

15. **Buddy Breathing Required.** Raise your right hand to collarbone height, palm toward your body, and point to your regulator or take your regulator out of your mouth and point to your mouth (buddy breathing is explained in detail on page 68).

16. **Stay There.** Raise your right hand to shoulder height, palm forward and fingers extended, like a traffic cop.

17. **Come Here.** Raise your right hand to shoulder height, palm back toward your body and fingers extended. Beckon slightly.

18. **How Much Air Do You Have?** (not pictured) Your instructor or dive guide points to his or her instrument console. Your response is to look at your air-pressure gauge and raise one finger for every thousand pounds you have left.

19. **Distress. Help!** This is a surface signal. Raise one hand high above your head to alert the boat crew that you need immediate assistance.

20. **I'm Cold.** Cross your hands in front of your chest, grabbing your upper arms with opposite hands to indicate chill.

(continued on next page)

🄼 Out of air.

🄵 Buddy breathing required.

🄶 Stay there.

🄷 Come here.

🄹 Distress, help.

🄺 I'm cold.

UNDERWATER LANGUAGE

• •

(continued from previous page)

21. **OK? OK.** These are surface signals to ask if another diver is all right and to reply that you are all right. If both hands are free, raise them both and bring them together at the top of your head to make a circle. If one arm is occupied, bring the other up in an arc and touch the top of your head.

22. **Under, Over, or Around.** This is an underwater signal to give intended direction to your buddy or dive pro. With your hand palm down, indicate your intended route to circumvent an underwater object or formation.

23. **Take It Easy. Slow Down.** Extend your hand in front of you, palm down, and make a "low" motion with it.

24. **Hold Hands.** Clasp your hands together in front of your chest.

25. **You Lead, I'll Follow.** With one hand out to the side and the other in front of your chest, point in the same direction with both forefingers.

21 OK? OK.

OK? OK (one arm occupied).

22 Under, over, or around.

23 Take it easy. Slow down.

24 Hold hands.

25 You lead, I'll follow.

• •

"**I** was diving with my brother and my niece, who is deaf. They were signing underwater. I realized that they were communicating and I couldn't. I've taken signing, but I can't always remember, so I developed cartoons to help divers sign underwater."

—Suzanne Kiffman, Sea Signs, San Diego, California

• •

Pool days

A classroom is a classroom is a classroom, and you're probably wondering what your first dive will feel like, so fast-forward to your first confined-water session. You will accomplish the following steps in a pool with the supervision of your instructor or dive guide.

• •

"**W**omen take to diving because they are patient enough to learn the concepts, and you have to grasp the concepts before you get around to the rest."

—Diane Richards, Rec Diving, Royal Oak, Michigan

• •

The fun really starts when you get wet. Before you earn your C-card, you need to learn the skills required to pass your certification test. These basics are learned in a swimming pool. You will use some of these skills every time you dive and they will eventually become second nature to you. Some of the other skills are ones you're unlikely to use in the normal course of diving, especially if you continue with escorted dive trips. If you haven't been diving for a while and have a trip coming up, sign up for a refresher course at your local dive center.

Setting up

Assembling the various pieces of equipment into an underwater life-support system is called *setting up equipment*, or simply *setting up*. On many dive boats, the crew will do this for you if you prefer, but learning to set up equipment is part of basic skills. In some classes, it's the first thing you learn at poolside. Your instructor or an assistant instructor should be on hand to guide you through this process and to answer questions. It's important to become accustomed to a particular sequence of actions so that when you're diving, you're unlikely to miss a step. The steps are as follows:

- Make sure the BC back straps are loose, then slide the tank into the strap loops on the back. The tank valve should be even with and opening toward the top of the BC. Tighten the straps. You can check if they are tight by lifting the BC by the shoulder straps. If you're able to lift the tank, the straps are tight. If the tank slips or stays on the floor, snug the straps down firmly.

● Remove the protective plastic cap (or protective tape) from the tank valve. Remove the plastic dust cap from the first-stage regulator, fit it onto the tank valve, and use the knob to screw it down tightly. Make sure the second stage is on the right side of the BC and the inflator hose and instrument console are on the left. Then release the knob slightly.

● Pull on the ring of the inflator hose and attach it to the inflator valve on the left side of the BC, pushing it up as far as you can; then release the ring. Check to make sure that it is snug. If the BC has Velcro straps or clips near the shoulder, you can batten down the hose.

● Holding the instrument console and second stage in one hand, slowly open the tank valve (i.e., turn it on) with the other hand. If you hear a hissing or leaking sound—especially where the first stage attaches to the tank valve—alert your instructor, who can check it and perhaps change the *O-ring*, which is supposed to protect against such leaks.

● When the tank valve is open, read the pressure gauge. Unless the instructor tells you that there is less air for these learning dives, the gauge should read about 2,500 psi.

● Press the purge valve on the second stage to make sure the air is flowing through it. Put it in your mouth and take a few breaths. Do the same with the octopus or auxiliary second stage.

● Carefully lay the tank—with the BC and regulator still attached—on its side. The pool deck isn't likely to sway the way a dive boat does, but this is a good habit to get into.

● Set up your weight belt. Your instructor will tell you how much weight you need. Some divers like to space the weights evenly; others like to have them in front, close to the buckle. Just don't put them on your back, under your tank, because that will be uncomfortable.

Setting up equipment includes attaching the first-stage regulator to the tank, and positioning it so that the primary-stage hose goes over your right shoulder and both BC inflator hose and instrument console are on your left side.

• •

"I am so unmechanical that anything more complicated than changing a light-bulb really throws me. I had an instructor who was a stickler for setting up right. He had me do it over and over. Everyone else was done, but I had to learn it, and finally I did. When I went on my first dive trip, I was the only woman who knew how to set up dive equipment. I helped some of the others, and I didn't make a single mistake. I was really proud of that."

—Debra Rowan, Fort Worth, Texas

• •

● Once you've set up, it's time to suit up. You may not be using a wetsuit in a warm pool, but once you begin diving, this is often the next step. (Some divers, however, prefer to put on their wetsuit before setting up their equipment.) Put on your weight belt and fasten it so that you can release it with your right hand. Your instructor or buddy will help you by holding the tank while you slip into your BC. Adjust the straps for comfort, making sure that the back of your head doesn't hit against the first-stage regulator (a common problem for short women). Get close to the edge of the pool and put on your mask, snorkel, and fins.

In a dive situation, you will double-check your buddy's gear and your buddy will double-check yours; often, the instructor or divemaster will recheck what you and your buddy have already checked and double-checked. Voilà! You're ready to get wet.

Into the water

When you start your confined-water dives, you will probably use a *seated entry*, which is the easiest and least intimidating. Sit down at the edge of the pool with your feet dangling in the water and the regulator in your mouth. Fill your BC about halfway. Slide forward slightly and, bracing yourself with your hands, rotate at the waist to twist your upper body. Place both hands on the pool's edge on one side of your body. Then pivot on your hands to swivel your body and lower yourself into the water. The seated entry can be used on a *boat dive* in calm water if the *dive platform* is close to the water.

As you progress through training, you will learn two more entries. To begin a *giant stride*, stand at the edge of the pool. Inflate your BC partway and put the regulator in your mouth. With one hand, hold your mask firmly against your face and the regulator in your mouth; with the other hand, hold onto the octopus and instrument console. Take one great big step, keeping your

This diver is getting ready for a giant stride off the platform of a dive boat by putting all her gear in place.

legs flared until you hit the water, then bring them together. Your inflated BC will bring you to the surface, where you can switch to your snorkel while waiting for your group to assemble before submerging. The giant stride is used often when entering the water from the dive platform on the stern of a dive boat and is almost always used when entering the water from a dock. It's important to learn to do this entry quickly, because divers are sent off the dive platform in rapid succession; anyone who stands there screwing up her courage to take the big step holds up everyone else.

You may not learn the *back-roll entry* in a confined-water class, but you will find it useful for diving from a small open boat. With your BC partially inflated, sit at the edge of the boat, with the regulator in your mouth and your back to the water. Press your regulator and mask against your face with one hand, and hold your instrument console and octopus in the other hand. Simply allow yourself to fall backward, raising your bent knees toward your body to make sure you clear the side of the boat. When you're in the water and on the surface, switch to your snorkel and wait for your group.

Down you go

No matter how you enter the water, once you're ready to descend, make the "OK" signal to your instructor and your buddy. When it's time for the group to submerge, raise your inflator hose as high above your head as you can and depress the deflator button at the top to vent the air from your BC. Alternatively, you can release the air by pulling on the dump-valve cord. In a shallow pool, you will begin to drift downward, but in open water (espe-

The **giant stride** is the most common entry into the water. You'll use it from the platform at the back of a dive boat or from a pier. Hold your mask and regulator against your face with one hand, and your gauges and loose gear against your body with the other. Take a giant step off the edge, keeping your legs in an open stride and your feet flat so that your fins break your fall as you enter the water.

cially salt water), you may need to kick downward to submerge. As you descend, pinch your nose with your thumb and forefinger and "blow your nose" sharply. This forces air into your ear and sinus cavities to equalize the pressure with the increasing hydrostatic pressure. This skill is crucial for comfortable and safe diving. This is called *equalizing*, or clearing your ears, and you'll do it every time you dive, from the shallowest dive to the deepest you ever make.

Buoyancy control

The next thing you will practice and practice and practice again is buoyancy control. The goal is to remain neutrally buoyant throughout your dive. Because various factors affect your buoyancy, as discussed previously, you need to learn to adjust the air in your BC to keep from unintentionally rising or sinking. Although you release all the air to descend, once you have leveled off, you need to add a little air to your BC to remain neutrally buoyant and to keep from touching bottom or descending too deep. Use the power inflator button on your inflator hose to do this, adding air one spurt at a time; it will be a few seconds until you're neutral again. As you breathe down your tank, you will have to continue adding air, a little at a time, to remain neutrally buoyant. There's not much to distract you in the pool except for your classmates' activities, so try to concentrate on these small adjustments and what they do. With experience, this becomes automatic. Oddly, when it's time to ascend, you must release the air from your BC and kick toward the surface to come up again (explained in the next section).

In addition to spending time practicing buoyancy control, paddling around admiring the tiles at the bottom of the pool, and getting accustomed to the fine, weightless feeling of being underwater, you will work with your instructor on a whole set of dive skills.

Mask clearing

One of the most important is called *clearing the mask*, which you need to do if a little water seeps in. Tilt your head back slightly, place your hand on the top of the mask frame at your forehead, and exhale sharply through your nose to expel the water. When you have cleared out the water, resettle the mask tightly against your face. If your mask features a purge valve, clearing is a push-button process; the manual method is nonetheless useful to know.

To **clear your mask**, tilt your head back so that you're looking upward. Press your hand against the top of your mask, so that the bottom of the mask pulls away from your face and at the same time, exhale sharply through your nose. This forces water out under the bottom of the mask. When the mask is clear, reposition it comfortably against your face.

You'll learn to clear your mask of just a little water that might seep in, and then you'll practice clearing it in *full flood*, a situation that could occur if your mask was completely dislocated or even knocked off—perhaps by the errant fin of a fellow diver. Your instructor will have you remove your mask, reposition it on your face, and then clear it completely. For many new divers, this is one of the scariest skills to practice, but how useful it is to have in your repertoire in case you ever need it.

Self-rescue skills

Other skills that you'll practice fall under the umbrella of *self-rescue skills*, meaning measures you can take to correct a mishap. Being competent and in control offsets the panic that might otherwise set in if you have a problem with your equipment. In addition to mask-clearing, these skills entail putting on and taking off one piece of gear at a time. You may never need to do this in a real dive situation, but these skills are an important part of every diver's basic training. You'll practice switching between your regulator and snorkel on the surface. Underwater, you will work on such skills as removing your mask and putting it on again, retrieving your regulator and putting it back in your mouth, taking your weight belt and BC off and putting them on again (although not at the same time!). You'll learn to keep breathing throughout each exercise, including exhaling slowly and steadily through your mouth while you remove and retrieve your regulator. You'll learn how to make a safe and controlled swimming ascent.

Ascending

When you're ready to ascend under normal diving conditions, you will learn to signal to your buddy that you're going up. When the signal is acknowledged, you both begin to ascend by kicking to propel yourselves toward the surface. Although not physiologically necessary in the pool, where you won't be making a safety stop, it's good practice to release any remaining air from your BC and kick upward to ascend. Unlike open water, where you'll stop at 15 feet for three minutes before surfacing, you can't make a safety stop on the way up from the bottom of the pool. In open water, if air remains in your BC, you would come up too fast as the remaining air expands. Similarly, there's no danger of coming up directly under a boat in a pool. However, even in confined water, you should get into the habit of raising one arm over your head as you approach the surface so you won't bang your head on some overhead obstacle in an open-water situation.

THE FIRST TEST

These basic skills may seem overwhelming, especially when you're reading them, but confined-water classes help you sort them out and turn them into habits. Once you have learned and practiced the fundamentals, you have to demonstrate them for your instructor. You also have to show minimal swimming ability. When I was getting certified, even before our scuba-skills test, we had to swim four laps in the pool and tread water for 10 minutes. I'm a really inefficient swimmer, no doubt a result of my Connecticut childhood spent horsing around in the Long Island Sound's choppy waters rather than learning proper swimming technique. As my scuba classmates were cruising in from their fourth lap, I was thrashing in from my third. The instructor evidently didn't notice and I chose not to point it out (although I have finally 'fessed up). The instructor cleared us for our four "open-water dives," which translates to running through those skills again in a sea, lake, or deep quarry waters. Because I went through the classroom and pool portions in Colorado in November, someplace tropical sounded really good for the open-water dives, which are the final step toward certification. So off I went to Hawaii with a referral in my pocket from my local dive shop to one in Kauai.

Chapter 5

INTO OPEN WATER

Your first open-water experience—in fact, at least your first *four* open-water experiences—will be part of the certification process, but merely getting out of the pool and into "real" water is a giant stride toward becoming a diver. For a beginner, that experience in itself is a thrill—or simply scary. Learning to handle yourself underwater and trusting your equipment goes a long way to allaying those fears. For other new divers, that first open-water dive—or the first dive trip to a beautiful place—fuels the fire of passion. No matter what, it will be memorable.

The road to becoming a scuba diver can be smooth, but for some of us, there are potholes. In fact, when you talk to dive enthusiasts about their early experiences, many admit that they felt afraid, even terrified, and overcame their fear to get certified. Some had trouble passing their skills tests but persevered. Their stories should be encouraging even during your most difficult moments. That's certainly what happened to me. I went through the classroom part with no problem. Some people freak when they submerge for the first time, all decked out in equipment that is awkward on land. Not I; I felt at ease from the get-go. As soon as I was underwater in the pool, I loved the feeling of subaquatic floating, and the skills were no problem at all. I took my confined-water training in Colorado and went to Kauai, Hawaii, for the final step.

Another beginner and I did our first two open-water dives in the warm, calm water off Poipu Beach. These were shore dives—walk-ins from the beach into a shallow, current-free cove.

Performing the skills to the instructor's satisfaction was as easy as in the pool, but the scenery was better. I cruised through them so quickly that there was plenty of time to explore. Even in water shallow enough to stand up in, bright little fish darted about, providing a preview of the marine world. Just two more dives to go for my C-card, I told myself, confident that I was home free.

THE HUMBLER

The next day was another situation altogether. I was the only beginner among a boatload of certified divers. A different instructor accompanied us. Our dive boat rolled and pitched

At the end of the dive, approach the ladder and hand your gear to the boat crew before scrambling back on board.

as we approached our dive site. Despite the rock-and-roll ride, my companions nimbly suited up while we were still underway. They listened to the instructor's briefing on the site and the depth and duration of the dive. Soon after we tied up to the mooring buoy, they jumped into the water and began to submerge, leaving only bubble traces on the water surface.

I went last. I clumsily moved onto the small platform affixed to the rolling, pitching boat's stern and stood there, terrified. I finally forced myself to take a giant stride into the water. As soon as I hit the water, one of my fins came off and floated down into what looked like a bottomless abyss. I hung onto the ladder on the dive platform, unsure of my next move. Then one of the other divers handed me the retrieved fin, which I wasn't so sure was a favor, for I was ready to bag the whole thing.

Still, I tried to put my fin back on with one hand, struggling to hang onto the ladder with the other. That didn't work, so I took off my other fin too, handed both up to one of the boat crew, and hauled myself up the ladder. Back on the still-moving platform, I got the fins back on and convinced myself to try again. I held my mask and regulator against my face and took another giant stride off the platform, this time dislocating a contact lens. I think the bottom of my mask must have pushed too hard against my cheek, which in turn scrunched up my lower eyelid. But that seemed a stupid reason to quit again.

I tried to ignore my Cyclops state and submerge, but the second try didn't go well either. This was the group's *deep dive*—to 95 feet—and between the surface and the seafloor, I had double nonvision. I couldn't see because that fuzzy blue zone is a featureless part of the ocean, and

KEEP THAT CARD

• • • • • • • • • • • • • • • • • • •

Hang on to your C-card, because without it, you won't be able to dive from a boat, rent gear, or have a tank filled. Certifying agencies charge $10 to $30 to replace a lost card, but the problem is, many of us don't know that it's lost until we're packing for a trip, at which point it's too late to get a replacement. Similarly, keep your logbook, in which you've recorded details of all your dives, in a place where you can find it when you're ready to go on a trip.

I couldn't see because of the dislodged lens. I got *really* scared. The instructor, who had been hovering near the surface to keep an eye on me and yet also watch the other divers far below, read the panic in my face and signaled for me to return to the boat. He was right. After all, he had to join the divers who knew what they were doing.

Dispirited and embarrassed, I clambered back aboard, repositioned my contact lens, and tried to console myself. Not being a certified scuba diver is hardly the end of the world. So what if I flunked because I hadn't been able complete four open-water dives? Confident that I'd have my certification, I had already made plans to join friends on The Big Island for some diving. In fact, just the day before, I had imagined telling them how easily my certification had gone. I reminded myself that, yes, I could find another dive shop on The Big Island and retake the open-water test there. It wasn't the way I had planned it, but it didn't matter all that much. Soon the others returned to boat, excitedly discussing the splendor of the dive site and the critters they had seen. My dejection deepened. I had wanted to be part of that group but, instead, I kept to my ignominious self as the boat headed for the second dive site.

• •

"For me, the scariest test was removing my mask underwater. I could do it in the pool, but doing it in the sea was the hardest skill I learned. I felt elated as I was waiting for the instructor to signal to go up. Just then, a giant manta ray swept overhead. He swam toward the shadows, then circled slowly and swam right over my head again. I looked up and saw his mouth, a large, black hole. Then he swam away. I remember thinking, 'Did that just happen?' Afterward, I learned it's not that common to see a manta ray."

—Elizabeth Glazner, Long Beach, California

• •

REDEMPTION

On a two-dive trip, it's customary to start with a shorter, deeper dive, followed by a longer, shallower one. Again, my companions hopped into the water with agility that I could only envy. I jumped in too, with less grace, but I did manage to hang onto everything and dislocate nothing as I submerged. Because the dive was just to 40 feet, the sun-dappled seafloor was visible from just beneath the surface. What a comfort! Instead of the featureless blue that I hadn't been able to penetrate on my first attempt, this dive site was bathed in warm light. It was easy to submerge to a bottom that I could see.

The instructor stayed with me as we drifted downward. At the sandy seafloor, he put me through my paces. I purposely had to flood my mask with water and clear it. Then I removed the regulator from my mouth and reinserted it, released my weight belt and rebuckled it, and performed all the skills as smoothly as I had in the pool at home and during the shore dives the previous day. And then, to be legal, the instructor had me repeat the entire repertoire. When I was finished, he made a circle with his thumb and forefinger to indicate "OK" and then beckoned me to follow him.

As we moved through the water, I was finally able to look around instead of concentrating on performing skills. For the first time, other than in photographs, I understood how the color *aqua* got its name, for the water was as green-blue and clear as on a travel poster. The benign sea caressed my skin. Beautiful reef fish, clad in scales of every color, swam through nature's own aquarium. The instructor led me to an underwater outcropping and pointed to a moray eel hidden in a crevice. I was in a world of wonder. Diving has given me a new perspective on nature's beauty, fragility, and resilience.

• •

"I signed up for dive classes with some friends. About my fifth dive, I was at the Blue Hole [a former quarry near Santa Rosa, New Mexico, where many Rocky Mountain dive shops conduct open-water dives]. A month later, I was in the Caribbean —St. Thomas, St. Croix, St. Lucia, the Dominican Republic. I touched a shark. I swam with turtles."

—Julie Welch, Cherry Hills, Colorado

• •

DIVE RIGHT

Although diving encompasses many specialties and locales, for the purpose of this chapter, assume the format is a day of diving from a commercial dive boat with a captain and at least one crew member, a dive instructor, and perhaps one or more divemasters or dive guides. The captain runs the ship, but the instructor is in charge of the divers. He or she will plan the dive, conduct a briefing outlining the dive profile, and perhaps tell you what you can expect to see below. Experienced divers, skilled in underwater navigation, often go off by themselves in buddy teams and then return to the boat. Beginning divers and their buddies usually are more comfortable—and wiser— following a pro.

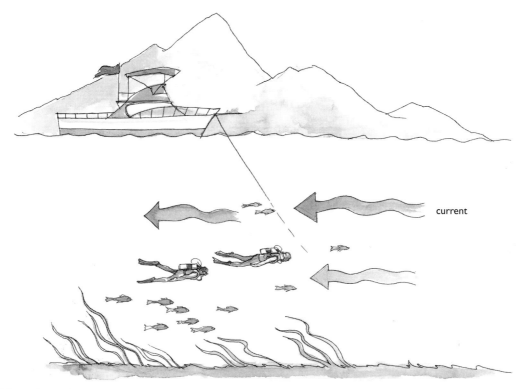

When swimming from a moored or anchored dive boat or a dock, you and your buddy should always head into the current, so that your return to the boat is with the current. Swimming against the flow consumes more air and is more tiring, but swimming with it aids your return to the boat or dock.

Boat dives fall into two basic categories. In the first, the boat is tied up to a permanent mooring buoy. (Except at a dive site with a sandy bottom where an anchor can do no damage, responsible dive operators use fixed buoys to protect the coral.) During the dive you might swim against the current to view the underwater attractions and return to the boat, or you may circle the spot where the boat is waiting. The crew may drop an additional bow or stern line, called an *ascent-descent line*, that drifts in the water and is a useful aid for both descending and for the safety stop during the ascent. (Club Med and some other dive boats drop two lines with a bar suspended between them 15 feet below the surface to help divers with their safety stop.)

The second type is a *drift dive*, during which the divers swim with the current and the boat follows the trail of divers' bubbles. When divers begin to surface, the boat picks them up. For many divers, drift-diving is the most pleasant of all, because swimming back against the current isn't required.

BUDDY UP

When you do your pool work, you may be assigned a buddy to get into the habit of pairing up, and you will practice some skills together. In fact, without a buddy, you can't practice *buddy breathing*, an emergency procedure in which two divers breathe off a single regulator and share air during a

• •

"**M**y first buddy on my first dive trip was a muscle man. He wanted to poke around in every hole and get personal with every fish. It made me nervous. On the next day's dive, I got buddied with another woman who was certified just a few months earlier. We took it easy and looked at a lot of little stuff close-up and kept out of holes. I had a great time, and she told me afterwards that she was happy to be showing someone the ropes."

—Lee Gardner, Fayetteville, North Carolina

• •

needed ascent—a situation that is uncommon now that most divers have an octopus as an alternate air source. However, in addition to buddy breathing and other drills that you perform together, you will also spend some of your pool time working one-on-one with your instructor, listening to directions while in a group, and practicing your skills in total self-absorption while your buddy does the same.

Once you begin diving, having a dive buddy, staying together, and paying attention to each other are required for good sense and safety. Spouses, partners, and friends who travel together make natural buddy teams, but if that isn't your situation, you will buddy up with a stranger on every dive trip. (Don't worry, you won't be strangers for long!) Ideally, conventional wisdom has it that dive buddies should share the same underwater interests and have roughly the same skill level. However, when you first start to dive, you may not know what your interests are and you may be happy to buddy up with a more experienced diver— and both of you may agree to stay close to whoever is leading the dive. During the briefing, the instructor also may say, "If you need me, remember that I'll be wearing big yellow fins" or "I'm the only one with a pink tank cover."

Buddies help each other before they even get into the

The first useful thing one buddy can do for another is to lift the tank while the BC is being buckled up. This is especially true in shore dives, such as this one at Colorado's Aurora Reservoir dive site, where there's no boat and therefore no boat crew to help.

water. You may lift each other's tanks to make it easier to slip into your BCs, and you perform visual checks of each other's equipment to ensure that everything is on and hooked up correctly. When you're in the water, waiting for the group to descend, you and your buddy will keep each other in sight. You'll keep an eye on each other on the way down. At the bottom, you should stay together—not glued together, but still within easy sight of each other. Not only is the buddy system a major part of diving safely, but having a buddy is also like having an extra pair of eyes. If one of you sees a great critter, it's good buddyhood to point it out.

When it's time to ascend, you and your buddy should do so together, staying together during the safety stop and surfacing at about the same time. If one of you runs low on air or has another problem and must go up before the planned end of the dive, try to alert the instructor or divemaster, and then ascend together. A buddy never lets a buddy surface alone in an emergency, unless an instructor or divemaster takes over the situation.

How to be a good dive buddy

- **Plan your dive.** The instructor or divemaster will brief you on the parameters of your upcoming dive (i.e., how long, how deep, how far). Within those parameters, you and your buddy should agree on what you want to do: Do you both like to stay close to the divemaster or are you competent to explore farther afield together? Do you prefer hovering close to the reef to see and perhaps photograph details, or do you like cruising around and covering more territory? Are your interests compatible? If you're a naturalist, you'll never want to buddy up with a spear fisherman (which, by the way, is rather unlikely during escorted dive trips).

- **Agree on a "comfort zone."** Again, within the parameters outlined by the instructor or divemaster, agree on maximum depth, bottom time, and where you will dive. Some divers, for instance, love exploring caves or lava tubes and have the training to do so, others can't stand the thought of being confined in what are called *overhead environments*. The dive must be tailored to the less skilled or the more cautious of the buddies.

• •

"I've always been a water baby, so when I started watching *Sea Hunt*, I was hooked —as were many people of my generation, but not a lot of women. I started scuba diving in the late 1960s, when I was in college. I was the only woman in a class of 25 led by a tough, retired Navy Frogman. I had to show everyone right away that I wouldn't whine when I was treated like one of the guys. My instructor and fellow divers were free to knock off masks, turn off air, jerk on fins, and generally harass each other into being comfortable with emergencies underwater. Learning to dive was a far cry from the supportive, encouraging experience of today."

—Dale Leatherman, Snowshoe, West Virginia

• •

- **Keep the buddy group small.** Usually, two divers comprise a buddy team. But when an odd number of divers is aboard a boat, one team will have three buddies. A family of four may wish to dive together; however, keeping track of any more than four people is daunting, so limit your group to that number.

Holding onto the anchor line or a stern line deployed for the purpose helps divers stay at 15 feet for the safety stop recommended on the ascent. This buddy team has stayed together from suiting up to the end of the dive.

- **Check each other before the dive.** When both of you are suited up and ready to dive, visually inspect each other's gear to make sure that everything is in place: gear properly hooked up, BC and weight belt cinched in, alternate air source tucked into a BC pocket, snorkel in place, and so on. The instructor, divemaster, or member of the boat crew may turn on your air to ensure there's enough in the *bottle* for the planned dive—and more, just as a contingency.

- **Check each other during the dive.** Keep each other in sight. Many buddies like swimming side-by-side; some even like to hold hands to make sure they stay in contact. Others take turns leading and following; however, the leader must listen for the sound of the follower's bubbles and look back frequently. If the follower needs to get the leader's attention, a gentle tug on a fin should do it.

- **Communicate.** Eye contact and clear hand signals are imperative to communicate (see pages 53–56). Avoid wild, random, or confusing gestures.

- **Calling a dive.** You and your buddy should agree that if either has reservations about safety, skills, conditions, or anything else other than beginner's edginess, it's OK to abort the dive—and that you will stay together until you're both on the surface and in sight of the dive-boat captain and crew. If you're the one who is nervous about diving or think you might want to come up, try to stay with an instructor or divemaster until you overcome your unease.

GETTING HOOKED

As you begin your open-water dives, remember that you have already familiarized yourself with the gear. You're diving with an instructor and perhaps a divemaster too. You enter the water,

An astonishing number of women describe themselves as "hooked" on diving—hardly surprising when you think of splendors such as these delicate fan corals, and other flora and fauna of the deep.

release the air from your BC, and begin to submerge (discussed in chapter 4). You find out what it feels like to be underwater and how important it is to equalize in order to adjust the air pressure in your ears as you descend in a real-dive situation. You also practice the fundamentals of buoyancy control in water deeper than the deep end of the pool. You perform the skills and, when you pass, you'll be an official diver—but getting certified is only the beginning.

Every dive is different, so the experience never gets old. If you're diving in warm water, the passing parade of small tropical fish changes from moment to moment. The scenery itself shifts as you move along. The sea fans, soft coral, and underwater vegetation flutter with the current, and the colors change as sunlight filters through the water. You may follow the group into the remains of a shipwreck. It's not a silent world, but it's essentially a nonverbal one. The most prevailing underwater sound is that of your own breathing. You'll hear the whoosh of your inhales and the rushing bubbles of your exhales. If you're a little nervous, the sound of your own respiration can be soothing. For some, it's more than that; it's a spiritual experience. In fact, you'll find that many of the best dive sites around the world have names like The Cathedral or The Temple.

Air-y matters

One of the signs of being a good diver is using air efficiently. Don't worry if you suck up a lot of air early in your diving career; nervousness may cause you to breathe rapidly or with shallow breaths. As you become more comfortable in the water, you can concentrate on breathing regularly, rhythmically, and deeply. Because women have smaller lungs with less air capacity, we tend to use less air than male divers of comparable ability.

Your tank will probably be filled with around 2,500 psi when you begin your dive. You can begin conserving air by using your snorkel when you're on the surface, waiting for the group to assemble for the descent. As you submerge, look at the instrument console to monitor your depth. You may notice the needle on the air-pressure gauge descending as rapidly as you do. Don't worry, it's normal to use a lot of air on the way down, especially to a deeper dive of 80 or 90 feet or more.

"**D**iving is the only religious experience I've had. It's the only place where I can really see God—quite clearly."

—Lauren Hutton, model, actress, and environmentalist

Keep your console in your left hand (no matter whether you're left- or right-handed) and monitor it frequently during your dive for both depth and air pressure.

Once you have reached your planned depth, take a moment to adjust the air in your BC so that you're neutrally buoyant—then off you go, with either just your buddy or in a group, following the instructor. Keep the instrument console in your left hand, whether or not you're left- or right-handed, and glance at it frequently to monitor depth and air consumption. Swim naturally and comfortably, kicking with your fins. Crawling or breaststroking with your arms for propulsion uses more air because it's not aerodynamically (or aquadynamically?) efficient. Swim steadily but don't race. A good, efficient body position is swimming with your torso about 10 or 15 degrees off horizontal, with your head slightly up and your feet slightly below your body. When you're properly weighted and your tank is adjusted correctly, that body position is not difficult to attain. It allows you to see where you're going and also to look down and to the side at the plants and animals below.

You use more air, more quickly, on a deeper dive than a shallower one, which is OK because a deep dive is always of shorter duration. You use more air if you are swimming against the current than if you are in still water or moving with the current. You use more air if you're wearing a thick wetsuit or a dry

TURKISH DELIGHT

• • • • • • • • • • • • • • • • • •

"My first dive was off the coast of Turkey during my honeymoon. I was scared. I thought I would drop to the bottom or run into a large creature like a shark. My blonde Australian female instructor, who strapped a knife on her leg, took me by the arm and down we went. Luckily, we went to a spot that was only about 30 or 35 feet in depth. I floated down without effort. It was so cool to be underwater and breathing—I couldn't get over that. I looked up a few times to see if there were any creatures about, but mostly I loved the feeling of gliding along so freely and gazing at all the wonderful plant life. It was exhilarating. Afterward, during lunch on the deck of the dive boat, I found out that the instructor had been catching tiny fish with her knife to use to lure a bigger fish. Then she was going to use the bigger fish to lure a moray eel out of its hiding spot. When she tried that ritual with me that afternoon, I had to use hand signals to say no way! I wasn't interested in meeting the moray. She probably thought I was a wimp, but she never said anything about that later."

—Iseult Devlin, outdoor writer,
Hoboken, New Jersey

The prospect of meeting a moray eel is enough to scare some new divers. Experienced divers tend to view morays as highlights of great tropical dive sites.

suit and, therefore, are more heavily weighted than in a dive skin or a lightweight shortie. A calm diver who swims subtly and aerodynamically, with her hands at her sides, uses less air than one who uses her arms to swim and thrashes around. Everything else being equal, a larger, more muscular diver uses more air than a petite diver. Instructors usually want divers to begin their ascent process when they have 1,000 psi in their tank and to surface with 500 psi remaining.

When it's time to surface, try to remain neutrally buoyant throughout the ascent. Hold the instrument console in your left hand and use it to monitor your ascent. With your body vertical, kick gently toward the surface. Thirty feet per minute is a good rate of ascent. Reestablish neutral buoyancy, make your safety stop at 15 feet for three minutes, then continue your ascent to the surface, breaking the water with an upraised arm. Inflate the BC halfway and switch from your regulator to your snorkel while waiting to get aboard the boat. If you want to remove your mask, pull it down around your neck rather than push it up on your forehead; the latter is considered a distress signal.

THE NEXT STEP

Once you have earned your C-card—and you have *truly* earned it— you can be thinking about what kind of diving you will do and where it will take you. You may be so enraptured that you immediately buy a full set of equipment because you have discovered that the rental gear you used during the learning and certification process doesn't cut it anymore. You may want to dive locally, which makes owning your own gear more economical than renting in the long run. Perhaps you will book a dive vacation to an excellent locale or plug diving into the next trip you already have planned.

Shopping list

Once you're committed to diving, it may be time to begin shopping. You probably already have your mask, snorkel, and fins, but they are listed here in case you're still renting or borrowing. You can buy one piece at a time and continue renting other pieces, or you can purchase everything at once. (See chapter 3 for detailed explanations of equipment.) Here are the items for your shopping list.

Must-have equipment

- Mask, snorkel, and fins (and booties for open-heel fins)
- buoyancy control device
- regulator
- exposure protection
- dive tables or planners
- *logbook* (dive diary)
- waterproof dive watch
- waterproof dive compass
- tank weight belt (supplied by dive operators, but mandatory)

Optional equipment

- dive light
- gear bag
- extra clips for attaching accessories to the BC
- soft weights
- dive computer and download kit to export data to the PC
- slate and marker
- defogging solution
- dry bag (for keeping equipment dry aboard the dive boat)
- spare parts (e.g., O-rings, extra fin straps, mask strap, goggle clip, silicone lubricant)
- knife or tool
- pony bottle or other *redundant air source*
- collecting or lift bag (only for locations where picking up shells, dead and broken coral, or artifacts is permitted)

A dive light allows you a better view of coral colors and details. It's also indispensable for night diving. Here, a diver illuminates anemone off the Seychelles Islands.

If you get interested in underwater photography, you'll have an array of waterproof photographic equipment to ponder.

- underwater camera with strobe (or waterproof housing for your camera)
- underwater communications device

Soft goods accessories

- dive hood (for cold-water diving)
- gloves
- Lube Suit (undersuit for getting in and out of a wetsuit more easily)
- "beach accessories" such as a big wrap-around towel, sunscreen, sunglasses, brimmed hat, and water bottle
- wind-resistant jacket to wear on the boat

Chapter 6

DIVING SAFELY

Diving can be the most beautiful and tranquil experience. After all, you immerse yourself in a spectacular environment and truly become one with nature. But diving is also intimidating because that environment is alien and you need a life-support system to operate in it. Just learning about equipment and basic diving technique, as well as discovering the sensations of breathing and moving underwater, is enough to take the edge off many new divers' fears. But there may be lingering doubts about the safety of scuba diving, and with good reason.

Although diving is statistically safe, when something goes wrong, it can go *very* wrong, *very* fast, which is why the entire dive industry—instructors, divemasters, dive guides, and certifying agencies—is so obsessed with safety. As a new diver, you might feel more secure following an instructor, divemaster, or dive guide until you have more entries in your logbook and experience under your weight belt. Meanwhile, be realistic about what alarms you and don't let harrowing tales of highly technical adventure diving keep you out of the water.

A macho cave-diver who pushes the envelope and dies while attempting a record-deep dive in a labyrinthine overhead environment makes headlines as surely as a climber who perishes on Mount Everest. Just as most people hike and climb mountains without incident, most divers have a great time without ever getting sick or hurt, let alone killed. Safe diving makes no headlines. As a diver, you don't want to make headlines—ever. However, it's smart to be alert to the dangers, which will inspire you to become a safe and conservative diver; that, in turn, will make diving a thrill and a pleasure for you. See Five Tips to Tune Up Your Skills on page 94 for a checklist of how to avoid making headlines and becoming an accident statistic.

WHEN NOT TO DIVE

Certain medical or physical conditions, whether chronic like diabetes and cardiovascular disease or as temporary as a head cold or pregnancy, mean that you either should not be underwater or only in controlled circumstances and under close medical supervision. The Divers Alert Network (DAN) is the primary conduit for information from the medical community to the dive community; contact DAN for specific questions (see chapter 10, Resources). *Always* check with a dive doctor or your own physician before beginning to dive—or if your health condition has changed. When in doubt about whether you should or shouldn't dive, be conservative. In some cases, going shallow is the answer; in others, you should snorkel instead. Following are some medical situations that should be red flags, rather than a red and white *dive flag*.

When you're sniffling

Diving with a cold or sinus condition is nothing to sneeze at, so don't go underwater, because you won't be able to equalize on the descent. Diving when your ears or sinuses are congested can therefore cause a condition called *ear barotrauma*. Many people try to combat congestion, especially in the early stages of a cold, with over-the-counter decongestants (in fact, some hard-core divers jokingly refer to Sudafed as "Vitamin S"). However, the medication might wear off while you still need it to handle the changing pressure during your dive, or the dosage might not be sufficient for you. (See Ear Problems later in this section.)

When you're dehydrated

Perhaps you're affected by jet lag or temporarily debilitated by a hot and humid climate or by the hot dry sun compounded by breathing dry compressed air. If you're simply not feeling well, think about skipping a dive or two. Rest and drink plenty of water to rehydrate—the next day's dive will be much better.

When you have recently undergone surgery

Divers want to know how soon they can dive again after operations ranging from brain surgery to hysterectomies. The simplest answer is "When you're completely healed," which means dive only with your surgeon's blessing. Again, conservatism is common sense in these circumstances.

When you're expecting

Because pregnant divers simply haven't taken the chances that would provide statistical or empirical data, no one really knows what effects water pressure at diving depths has on a developing fetus.

No one wants to put her baby's health at risk for the sake of a few dives. Obstetricians generally recommend that a woman wait at least four weeks after a vaginal delivery to resume diving. After a cesarean section, the same "when fully healed" guideline as for any other surgical procedure applies.

If you have heart disease

The most common cause of noninjury fatalities in male divers over 30 and female divers over 40 is cardiovascular disease. If you have this problem, don't dive. Period.

If you're diabetic

Insulin-dependent diabetics were long warned not to dive as a precaution against suffering a hypo- or hyperglycemic incident underwater. Recent research indicates that diabetics who are closely monitored—in terms of both diving and blood-sugar highs and lows—can dive in controlled situations and under medical supervision. If you have a physician who is a diver, you have a better chance of a reasonable evaluation of your situation, rather than a blanket proscription against diving.

If you have respiratory problems

Because diving involves breathing in the unnatural situation of using compressed air, lung problems often red-flag diving. Emphysema and other severe, chronic respiratory problems do not mix with scuba diving. Some authorities also believe that asthmatics should not dive, although others believe that diving is only hazardous within 48 hours of an attack. Opinions differ not only on whether asthmatics may dive, but—even among those who feel it's OK—also about people who have outgrown childhood asthma versus those who developed the condition in adulthood, as well as how much medication is required to control it. Again, your own physician—or a doctor who dives—can give you the best answers.

Of course, that there are answers to all your concerns doesn't mean diving is risk-free. Its dangers are real and the consequences of a mistake can be serious. However, when you practice those skills that you learned at the outset during every dive, it's one of the safest sports.

WHAT CAN GO WRONG

Some of the things that can go awry in your scuba diving experiences involve the element of exotic travel, which seduces many people to become divers in the first place. Lost luggage, missed airplane connections, jet lag, and *turista* are obstacles that many travelers have to overcome, whether or not they are divers. Since some of the best diving takes place in exotic locales—often in developing countries—the odds are pretty good that you will encounter at least one of the obstacles. On a dive trip to Virgin Gorda in the British West Indies, I flew from Denver via Miami and San Juan; my bags ended up in Chicago, where they languished for a couple of days before

• •

"My beau and I took a dive trip to Honduras. Sounds idyllic, but we had to take six flights to reach the tiny island of Guanaja, named after its pine trees. Unfortunately, Hurricane Mitch left no pine needles or foliage on any of the island's trees. The resort was in disrepair and had financial hardships because of the dearth of post-Mitch tourism. To make things worse, the airline had sent our luggage to Guatemala. My friend got scuba-certified, but he also got seasick. Still, the trip was romantic, exciting, and challenging, and that's what makes the best trips."

—Annemarie Leon, Boulder, Colorado

• •

catching up with me. My clothing bag eventually reached me intact, but my tattered gear bag by that time contained two fins and one bootie. Period. Was it inconvenient? Certainly. Was it harmful? Not really. Lost or damaged luggage can happen to any traveler; on a dive trip, you can usually rent replacement gear at your destination.

Sunburn, dehydration, and even heat stroke can affect people in the tropics, whether or not they dive. However, there are other problems endemic to diving; some are underwater emergencies, others manifest themselves later, at the surface. When a problem occurs underwater, whether it is yours or your buddy's, stop and respond to the situation. Keep breathing regularly and see that your buddy is doing so too. Think about ways to solve the problem. You will have practiced many self-rescue and buddy skills, and now is the time to put a suitable one into practice. Obviously, it makes sense to alert an instructor, divemaster, or guide if you can, but don't get in the habit of relying on someone else to solve your problems. Dive instructors often remind their students: "Stop. Breathe. Think. Breathe. Act. Breathe."

Following are some problems that could arise on a dive trip and what to do about them.

Seasickness

You might feel queasy on the Staten Island Ferry or be able to cross the Drake Passage without a hiccup, but if you get seasick on a dive trip, it might hit you even before you reach the first dive site. If you know you're susceptible, take a precautionary pill. Dramamine is the best-known medication, but other over-the-counter and prescription medications are available too. You're unlikely to doze off while diving, but ask for a brand that doesn't cause drowsiness. Transdermal patches, which resemble round Band-Aids and are worn behind the ear, help some people, but they aren't ideal for underwater use. Other people prefer Sea-Bands—elastic bracelets worn on the wrist at an acupressure point—for nausea. Ginger is said to relieve nausea too. Other people just take the practical approach. If they feel seasick, they give in to it, vomit once, and get it over with—usually joking that they are chumming for good fish. (If you continue to feel nauseated underwater, remember that regulators are designed to pass anything you expel through the mouth.)

Ear Problems

Sniffles, minor colds, sinusitis, and allergy outbreaks—all conditions that block the passages between your sinuses and ears, which aren't worth fussing about on land—can prevent you from equalizing; therefore, they are a temporary red flag to diving. Decongestants have been known to wear off in mid-dive. The first rule is to equalize throughout your descent and to not continue if you can't equalize. Even if

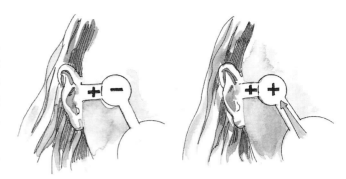

As the hydrostatic pressure increases during the descent, you will begin to feel discomfort (left). When you equalize, you force air into your inner ear, and the discomfort goes away (right). You must equalize to dive comfortably and avoid permanent damage to your ears.

you manage to equalize on the descent, you might feel the pressure in your ears or sinuses on the ascent. This is known as *reverse block* or *reverse squeeze*, or more technically as *ear barotrauma*. An ear infection, which can be a residual from a cold, should also keep you on the surface—and probably send you scuttling to a doctor's office. With the sole exception of a new type of vented earplug designed to enable divers to equalize (see chapter 10, Resources), never wear earplugs while diving.

Toothache

You might not know that you have an abscessed tooth or simply a poor filling until you ascend and feel severe pain inside a tooth, also called *dental barotrauma*. You can equalize your ears but there's no way to equalize a tooth. The only solution is to continue to ascend and then go see a dentist; the best prevention is to have a dental checkup before a dive trip.

Mask squeeze

Mask squeeze usually occurs during rapid descents to depth if a diver isn't careful about equalizing the airspace inside the mask. If you have unequal pressure there, the mask can press too tightly against your face, causing temporary swelling or even bruising. This condition may look bad, but it's not really serious. The same procedure that you use to equalize your ears—that is, holding your nose between thumb and forefinger and trying to exhale through your nose—generally equalizes your mask as well as your ears. Underwater nosebleeds, which can be related to mask squeeze, are not unknown. A nosebleed also looks bad, especially if you find blood in your mask when you surface, but it isn't serious.

Stings and bites

Critters that sting, bite, or secrete irritating venom when touched are part of the maritime environment, especially in the tropics where, ironically, you may prefer to dive in a shortie wetsuit without gloves. This is nature's way of reminding us undersea interlopers to look but don't touch. Some organisms are attached to the seafloor or underwater rocks and may look like mild-mannered

One way to avoid abrasions or rashes from toxins secreted in some undersea organisms is to wear a full-length exposure suit, even in tropical waters, and avoid touching anything. This diver has her hands on the coral, but at least she's wearing gloves to protect her hands and minimize the impact on the coral.

undersea plants. Yet, if you touch them, you'll feel a burning or itching sensation and perhaps develop an impressive rash or blisters at the contact area. In many cases, a topical antitoxin lotion or antihistamine will alleviate the worst symptoms.

Beautiful as they are, anemones, fire corals, fire sponges, and stinging hydroids are among the common culprits. Spiny sea urchins, by contrast, look as ugly as they are unpleasant. These small black balls are surrounded by thorn-like spikes that are several inches long. Like fishhooks, they pierce the skin easily, but they break off and are painful to pull out. Spiny urchins are found in tropical shallows, often at snorkeling or even wading depths. The crown-of-thorns starfish can grow to 24 inches in diameter, and each of its dozen or more arms is covered with short sharp spines that secrete a toxic substance. Scorpionfish, stonefish, and lionfish are ugly yet fascinating, camouflaged to blend with their environment, and venomous. Saltwater catfish have black and white stripes along their bodies, swim in schools, and feature a venom gland on their backs.

The deadly venom of sea snakes, which are found in the Indian and Pacific oceans, reputedly is 20 times as potent as cobra venom. Sea snakes can grow to 6 feet long, propelling themselves through the water with their squished-down tails that function almost like tailfins. Bristleworms, often 6 inches long, come in beautiful colors but pack a painful sting. Various types of jellyfish secrete toxic venom, some worse than others. The real villain of the ocean is the Portuguese man-of-war, which floats on the surface while its near-transparent tentacles dangle in the water below. They have the worst sting.

"Sea lice" is the all-purpose name given to something unseen that causes irritation. It can be a small, free-floating organism or parts broken off from some other toxic critter. Sea lice are insidious and unpleasant. In contrast to these nasty little buggers, such "menacing" animals as sharks, eels, octopus, squid, and barracudas rarely, if ever, attack divers.

Gas

It's not uncommon to feel some discomfort in your stomach or intestines during the ascent, as the air in your digestive tract expands. Dive officialdom delicately refers to it as *abdominal squeeze* or *abdominal barotrauma*. Most of the time, it passes easily—think of it simply as expelling two sets of bubbles—and, unlike topside social situations, other divers won't even notice.

Out-of-air emergency

This shouldn't happen, but it could. The first rule is to either try to alert your buddy or the dive instructor, divemaster, or dive guide (use the palm-down, "throat-cutting" signal), who can give you an octopus, or to use the buddy-breathing techniques you practiced in class. If that is impossible for some reason, you will need to make an emergency ascent and kick for the surface—another skill you practiced in class. Dump your weight belt, but keep the regulator in your mouth even if you think you're out of air—the air expanding in your tank as you rise toward the surface may provide another few breaths. The regulator not only enables you to keep water out of your mouth, but it also lets you exhale slowly as you ascend to avoid lung overexpansion (see page 85). When you get to the surface, breathe through your snorkel and raise one arm overhead in an arc; this signals an emergency situation to the dive boat. By now, your buddy and/or an instructor should have noticed your plight and come to stay with you.

Decompression sickness (DCS)

This is the biggie when it comes to diving danger. Its street name is the bends, it hurts like hell, and the potential seriousness of the condition is severe. Here's what it is: the compressed air that you breathe underwater is a combination of oxygen and nitrogen, an inert gas. While you're diving, your body dissolves and stores nitrogen. The deeper you dive or the longer you're underwater, the more nitrogen you will accumulate. While you're at diving depths, the water pressure "holds" the nitrogen.

As you ascend, that pressure is lessened, which causes the nitrogen to coalesce into tiny bubbles that reside in your tissues and blood vessels. If you dive conservatively, stay well within the no-decompression limits, are conscientious about your safety stop (see page 52), and are mindful of the proper surface interval between dives, you will eliminate the excess nitrogen naturally. However, if you ascend too quickly or come to the surface without the safety stop, the gas comes out of solution more quickly than you can eliminate it, resulting in DCS. Think of it as shaking up a soda bottle—those small bubbles that were "under control" when the bottle was in the refrigerator will fizz up. Visualize DCS as a similar "fizzing" of the excess nitrogen in your body. Furthermore, if you exercise vigorously before you eliminate the residual nitrogen, you will heat it up and intensify the DCS effect, as if you put the soda bottle in the hot sun and then shook it up.

Experts note that half of all DCS cases become evident within an hour after diving, most occur within 12 hours, but some do not show up until 36 hours later. This is why you have to wait at least 24 hours after diving before boarding an airplane. Even pressurized jets are adjusted to the equivalent of about 6,000 feet above sea level, and small commuter airplanes used from a small island airport to a larger jetport nearby might not be pressurized at all. In any event, about 75 percent of DCS cases involve joint and limb pain—not fatal, but certainly miserable. Another non-serious version shows up as red rash-like patches, often on the shoulders and chest—but this type may mask more serious DCS that accompanies it. If the bubbles reach the brain or lungs, the situation is serious. Symptoms of DCS can be either mild or moderate and, therefore, easy to

WOMEN AND THE DCI RISK

• • • • • • • • • • • • • • • • • • •

"Are women at greater risk of experiencing decompression illness while menstruating? Theoretically, it's possible that because of fluid retention and tissue swelling, women are less able to get rid of dissolved nitrogen. This is, however, not definitely proven. One recent retrospective review of 956 women divers with DCI found 38 percent were menstruating at the time of their injury. Additionally, 85 percent of those taking oral contraceptives were menstruating at the time of the accident. This suggests but does not prove that women taking oral contraceptives are at increased risk of DCI during menstruation. Therefore, it may be advisable for menstruating women to dive more conservatively, particularly if they are taking oral contraceptives. This could involve making fewer dives, shorter and shallower dives, and longer safety stops."

—Donna M. Uguccioni, M.S.; Dr. Richard Moon, DAN Medical Director; and Dr. Maida Beth Taylor, "DAN Explores Fitness Diving Issues for Women," *Alert Diver* (Jan./Feb 1999)

dismiss, or so severe that it's clear that immediate attention is necessary. DCS symptoms include the following.

- breathing difficulty
- dizziness
- joint or limb pain
- numbness
- paralysis
- shock
- tingling
- weakness

Even if you conscientiously dive within those all-purpose, one-size-fits-all no-decompression limits, be aware that the following factors can inhibit your ability to release excess nitrogen and make you more susceptible to DCS.

- age
- alcohol consumption before or after diving
- altitude (high-altitude lake diving without dive-table adjustments)
- cold
- dehydration
- exercise (vigorous) before, during, or even after diving
- fatigue
- illness
- injury
- menstruation and/or oral contraceptives (see sidebar)
- obesity
- smoking/tobacco use

Divers who regularly experience discomfort, especially older divers, sometimes have luck with *enriched air*, also called *nitrox*, a mixture that usually contains 32 to 36 percent oxygen (as opposed to nature's 20 percent). Nitrox decreases the risk of DCS, and some divers report that enriched air makes them more energetic, keeps them warmer and more alert, and combats the dry-mouth effect of breathing compressed air through a regulator. Nitrox does require additional training to use.

Rescue divers, dive instructors, and other advanced-level divers are trained to deal with DCS. First aid, while still on the dive boat, includes administering oxygen to

Many conditions which preclude diving shouldn't keep you from enjoying the water. Snorkeling or skin diving in shallow water can be mesmerizing in its beauty.

help speed up the process of eliminating excess nitrogen. If it happens to you, you will be asked to lie on your left side with your head slightly elevated as you take the oxygen. The diver emergency center at most major dive destinations also operates a *hyperbaric chamber* for recompression, which helps the body gradually absorb and eliminate the nitrogen bubbles. You probably won't ever need this service (few recreational divers do), but it's comforting to know that a chamber is nearby.

Lung overexpansion

Here's another condition that is potentially serious, so pay attention. Overexpansion of the lungs, caused when a diver holds her breath during the ascent, can cause real trauma. Here's the reason. Remember that your regulator is designed to deliver air to you at the same pressure as the hydrostatic (i.e., water) pressure around you, which maintains normal lung volume while you're at depth underwater. If you breathe steadily and normally as you ascend, the regulator continues to readjust the air pressure to the changing hydrostatic pressure.

If you hold your breath as you ascend, the air pressure in your lungs becomes greater than the hydrostatic pressure, and they can overexpand during the ascent. An overexpanded lung won't burst or explode, but it can tear or rupture, causing the diver to cough up blood. Dive physicians have divided lung expansion into four specific types of injuries. Most are not life-threatening and are treated in much the same way as DCS. However, an air embolism or arterial gas embolism, in which a trapped air bubble from the injured lung enters the bloodstream or chest cavity, can be serious. Although it rarely happens, the bad news is that it could cause paralysis or death. The good news, however, is that prevention is easy and natural: breathe, breathe, breathe throughout the dive. Breathe even if you're thrilled (that is, don't let the breathtaking underwater scenery literally take your breath away). Breathe even if you're frightened. In other words, exhalation is the natural way to prevent reverse squeeze on your lungs.

Divewear like this, while flattering, can only be worn in the tropics. For colder waters, a thicker suit that covers more of the skin surface is necessary to avoid hypothermia.

Nitrogen narcosis

Another scary-sounding condition is a functional impairment called *nitrogen narcosis,* which has been likened to the effects of alcohol. Nicknamed *rapture of the deep,* it occurs when a diver reaches what is called the "narcotic zone." It rarely affects recreational divers, who dive no deeper than 130 feet and stay at that depth only briefly. Symptoms include a slowdown of thinking, acting, and paying attention to what's going on. Diving under the influence of too much nitrogen is similar to driving under the influence of alcohol. Both are bad ideas.

While most recreational divers never reach the depths at which nitrogen narcosis occurs, taking sedatives, barbiturates, sleeping pills, antidiarrhea medications, antimotion sickness medications, and others—especially in combination with alcohol—can decrease the depth at which the condition kicks in. One smart way to evaluate the effect that over-the-counter drugs have on bringing about nitrogen narcosis is to begin your dive trip with shallower depths, only going deeper on later dives if no problems occur.

Oxygen toxicity

Like DCS and nitrogen narcosis, *oxygen toxicity* is highly unlikely for those who dive conservatively within the *recreational dive tables.* If you go for nitrox dive training to use oxygen-enriched air (see page 85), you will be alerted to this potential problem. Oxygen toxicity can affect your lungs and central nervous system, but again, recreational divers rarely experience it.

Body-temperature problems

Even warm tropical waters are cooler than the 98.6°F normal body temperature, so prolonged immersion without exposure protection can eventually cause your core temperature to drop. Warm-water divers don't normally have any problems other than discomfort and chilling, but diving in anything other than tropical waters requires serious exposure protection (see pages 42–44). A less-anticipated issue is becoming overheated, called *hyperthermia.* This can occur during or even after a dive, because the wetsuit that kept you cozy underwater becomes a sauna suit when you're on the boat, in the sun.

Hyperthermia, also called *heat exhaustion,* occurs when the body cannot cool down to 98.6°F. The signs are heavy perspiration, weak breathing, rapid pulse, and cool skin, perhaps compounded by nausea and weakness. If not attended to, the result can be heatstroke, the symptoms of which are hot, flushed skin and a continued rapid pulse. The worst-case scenario is brain and systemic damage, even death. You can avoid overheating by setting up your gear before zipping on your wetsuit, removing it, or at least unzipping it, after diving, and by limiting your movements while you're zipped up—and, of course, by trying to stay out of the sun.

The opposite of heat exhaustion is hypothermia, which happens when the body cannot warm up to 98.6°F. The main sign is uncontrollable shivering; other symptoms include disorientation and problems with speaking, standing, or walking. If not attended to, the condition worsens, blood pressure drops—even as blood rushes to the skin (away from the organs)—and the victim feels overheated while the core temperature continues to drop. A warm, dry blanket or a hot-water bottle is enough to cure mild hypothermia; a severe case requires medical attention.

Drowning

Drowning is the leading cause of scuba-related deaths—and near-drowning can be one of the scariest things to happen to a human being, diver or not. The most common form of drowning is wet drowning, from water inhaled into the lungs. Rescue, resuscitation, first aid, and medical attention are called for. Dry drowning occurs when the larynx constricts and cuts off breathing.

EMERGENCY!

This isn't a first-aid book and, as a beginning diver, you should leave emergency procedures to the pros—stay out of the way unless you're asked to help. If you want to be able to respond to dive crises, continue your training and become a rescue diver. Meanwhile, remember that instructors and other advanced divers are trained in how to deal with emergencies, both in the water and once the victim is back on the boat. If a crisis occurs, fight your inclination to play Florence Nightingale—unless you are a doctor, nurse, EMT, paramedic, Red Cross–certified lifeguard, or other practitioner who can truly help.

HOW LOW CAN YOU GO?

Many of the terrible situations divers can find themselves in carry the caveat "Recreational divers who dive conservatively within dive tables are highly unlikely to encounter this situation." You will study, restudy, review, and re-review your dive tables, and you may learn to use a dive computer to do the calculations. But it's good to know the general parameters of various types of diving within the context of problems that could occur. *Deep diving* is not an absolute. In the early years of the sport, it was defined as anything below 50 feet. That has now been modified, and your first C-card is effectively a license to dive to 60 feet. However, as my first failed open-water dive proved, dive operators don't always stick to that number. As you become more experienced, you'll often dive from 80 to 100 feet on the first dive of the day. Later, especially if you go for advanced certification, you might go as deep 130 feet, which is considered the limit for general recreational or sport diving.

Diving any deeper than that is highly technical and specialized, often using *mixed gases* not found in nature, and *decompression* stops in order for the body to eliminate the accumulated excess nitrogen. This kind of advanced diving is way beyond the parameters of this book. Recreational diving is known as *no-decompression diving* because a lengthy decompression stop on the ascent is not necessary. To underscore its importance to your health, however, think of the safety stop as a mini-decompression stop. Although a safety stop is not physiologically imperative, it's an effective way of helping your body rid itself of excess nitrogen.

In theory, it's possible to do a single, short, no-decompression dive to a maximum of 190 feet but, in practice, sport diving takes place within 130 feet of the surface—and most of it is much shallower than that. As indicated previously, you will be combining a short deep dive, a longer shallow one, or something in between. If you're making a single dive in a day, these are the no-decompression limits—in other words, the maximum time you can spend underwater:

No-Decompression Limits

Depth in Feet	Single-Dive No-Decompression Limit in Minutes	Depth in Feet	Single-Dive No-Decompression Limit in Minutes
To 30	—	80	40
35	310	90	30
40	200	100	25
50	100	110	20
60	60	120	15
70	50	130	10

If you're doing more than one dive a day, you'll use dive tables that establish the combination of depth, duration, and surface interval between dives to keep you within safe limits. Dive computers are designed to perform those algorithmic calculations for you.

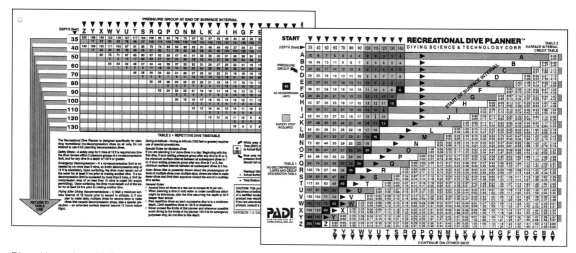

Dive tables, such as this Recreational Dive Planner, indicate how deep you can dive, how long you can stay down, and what your minimum surface interval must be before your next dive.

COVER YOURSELF

You probably don't drive a car without adequate insurance. Your house is insured against fire, theft, liability, and a variety of natural disasters. If you have dependents, you probably carry life insurance. You may also purchase short-term policies for travel or other situations. If you're a diver, you should carry dive insurance. The Divers Alert Network serves many functions in diving (see chapter 10, Resources, for contact information), the best known of which is insurance. In addition, DAN serves as the umbrella organization for dive safety issues and research. Its affiliated doctors, physiologists, and researchers are at the cutting edge of collecting, analyzing, and disseminating information and data concerning the effects of diving on the human body.

DAN is the safety watchdog for divers everywhere, but most recreational divers join for its insurance program and emergency hotline, which has answered more than 22,000 calls on medical issues from its inception in 1981 through 1999. The hotline is staffed by four full-time medics who dispense advice, suggest courses of emergency treatment for severe situations, and arrange for medical evacuation and hyperbaric-chamber referrals, when needed. You can also obtain dive insurance through individual certifying agencies.

Chapter 7

YOU'RE CERTIFIED —NOW WHAT?

Certification may have been your first diving goal, but it's just the beginning of your life as a diver. Think of it as "commencement" rather than "graduation." While you're working on the certification process, your diving attention is very focused. You need to concentrate on the chapter in the manual, the video on the monitor, and the skills and drills in the water. Once you have your C-card in hand and have gotten past the initial surge of satisfaction with your accomplishment, you may still find yourself overwhelmed by the myriad options that await you as a certified diver.

No question about it: the scuba world is confusing. Your Discover Scuba or other try-before-you-buy experience—and even the entire certification process—will have touched only the surface of an ocean-sized realm of organizations, equipment, skills, places to dive, and even names of diving celebrities. When you listen to divers' "scubatalk," log onto a scuba chat room on the Internet, or pick up a glossy dive magazine, it seems that you alone are still clueless about the dive world.

Once you have your C-card, the best thing you can do is get more "bubble time." You already know the several options you have on how to continue diving. Whether on a commercial dive trip (which is a wise and convenient choice for a novice) or an independent trip, you will buddy-up with another certified diver. If you're traveling with a mate or a friend, it's natural for you to be buddies. If you're both newly certified, let the instructor or dive guide know that neither of you has a lot of experience and that you will be sticking close by.

If you're traveling solo, the instructor or guide will match you up with a buddy. It's the fortunate novice who is teamed up with a more experienced diver; however, experienced divers usually try to buddy-up with each other. Another option on a commercial dive trip is to join a small group headed by the instructor or guide, who knows just where that moray eel is probably hiding or who can lead you to the most interesting part of the underwater wreck—and who can be there for you if you're still nervous about a new situation. "I'm going to be the one chewing on your fin," I told the instructor who led the first dives I made after I got certified. My buddy and I followed closely for that extra measure of security.

> "As students, women pay more attention. As instructors, they have more empathy. As divers, women have more patience. They'll stay on the reef and look at little stuff. Men want to see everything."
>
> —Stan Margolis, dive instructor on the island of St. Kitts

Technically, your C-card even allows you to get your own tank filled at a dive center but, in reality, few newly certified divers do. It may be your eventual intention, but the wise novice diver takes things one step at a time. The more you dive, the more comfortable you will feel underwater. Your goal should be to become self-sufficient and self-reliant—with your buddy, of course. Remember that a little hand-holding in the beginning is OK.

Once you're hooked on diving and you want to continue increasing your skills, you can sign up for the specialty courses. Or, like me, you can simply stumble into further levels of certification. The agenda of my first postcertification dive trip to the British Virgin Islands included a night dive. "Don't you need to be an Advanced Open-Water Diver for that?" I naively asked the

> "What makes a *good diver*? Is it the guy who swims the fastest? The woman who can hold her breath the longest? Or possibly the diver who is the most fearless . . . ? I've seen speedsters, breath-holders, and daredevils who could achieve unbelievable feats in the water, but they still weren't good scuba divers. On the other side of the coin, some divers are just average when it comes to physical prowess, but in the water they have that special look about them. They move slowly, use the correct technique, and are aware of what's around them, always at peace with their aquatic surroundings. They appear comfortable and confident—at ease in the water and sure of their own skills."
>
> —Lynn Laymon, in "Watermanship: The First Step to a Career in Diving," *Dive Training* magazine (Nov. 1996)

MYTHS AND MISCONCEPTIONS
• •

Myth: Now that I'm certified, my qualification to dive is good for life.
Fact: Although your certification card bears no expiration date, your qualification to dive may not be good for life.

Myth: With the advent of dive computers, there's no longer a need to understand dive-table theory.
Fact: Understanding the concept behind the dive tables and being able to calculate profiles are as important now as they ever were.

Myth: Sharks are dangerous to divers and should always be avoided.
Fact: Sharks have a lot more to fear from humans than we do from them.

Myth: In contrast to flying after diving, diving after flying poses no problems for divers.
Fact: Rushing to strap on a scuba tank as soon as possible after flying to a dive destination may increase susceptibility to DCS.

Myth: A safety stop is the same as a decompression stop.
Fact: Although every [recreational] dive can be considered a no-decompression dive, safety stops and decompression stops are not interchangeable terms.

—Linda Lee Walden, writing in *Dive Training* magazine (Nov. 1998)

trip leader. "No, but it's one of the requirements," he replied. So I participated in the night dive, enchanted by the iridescent critters that reminded me of fireflies on a summer night and fascinated by the night-feeders that we saw in the beams of our dive lights. With one of the skill elements out of the way, it seemed to make sense to go through the entire process. Even when I had my new card, I didn't consider myself an advanced diver and I still proceeded cautiously. Because I am a writer who dives, not a diver who writes, I don't dive as much as I'd like, so I still don't consider my skills to be at as high a level as I someday hope to achieve.

UNDERWATER ADVENTURES

You may live close to the water and dive locally—whether in the clement seas of Florida or rougher, colder waters of more northerly oceans or lakes. Early in your diving career, you should be honing your skills to be a safe, comfortable, efficient, and environmentally conscientious diver. In this section, I describe some of the wonderful experiences that highlight dive trips to tropical locations, where it's easier and more comfortable to refine your skills.

Two of the golden rules of conscientious diving are to keep your hands to yourself and to secure your loose gear close to your body. Wherever you go, don't get so excited at what you're seeing that you forget to practice buoyancy control—and remember to keep your hands off the coral reefs and away from the critters. A loose octopus or instrument console that smacks against a coral formation or drags over a marine plant can damage it. No matter what you see at theme parks, you won't be able to latch onto a dolphin, and it would be an abuse to a wild creature if you did. Remember too that hitching a ride on a turtle or fondling a fish can traumatize the marine animal. Some organisms and animals secrete toxic substances that are pos-

Don't hitch a ride on a passing dolphin or turtle, but that doesn't mean that one won't come over to make friends with you.

itively nasty to your skin (see page 81). Don't worry; you'll still have plenty of time to look around at the splendors of the deep.

As you read chapter 6, which outlined virtually everything that could possibly go wrong, you may have begun to have doubts about diving. Some women learn to dive to prove something to themselves or to please a partner, but the main reason that many women continue to dive is that the underwater world is filled with such incredible beauty and wonder. Here, in no particular order, are some of the experiences you will have and environments in which you can dive.

Watching marine life

I have never experienced the physiological rapture of the deep, but every time I dive in a beautiful place, I feel what I think of as emotional and aesthetic rapture of the deep. Drifting beside a massive coral head assembled micro-animal by micro-animal into a towering undersea sculpture; swimming amid a school of brilliant reef fish and pretending to be a bigger fish; threading through an undersea arch from one spectacular under-seascape to another; hovering near a sandy seafloor as seemingly aircraft-carrier-sized manta rays swoop overhead; coming face-to-face (or mask-to-snout) with a sea lion; flirting with a grouper; or watching the balletic grace of an octopus moving in the beam of a dive light is to feel awe, reverence, and wonder at the magnificent world beneath the waves.

The nonverbal aspect of diving intensifies these feelings. You can point out something special to your buddy or you can look at something another diver points out to you, but the experience won't be cluttered with superficial verbiage. Instead, you find yourself concentrating more so that you can share the thrill of the experience once you're back on the surface.

Spotting various fish species is the submarine equivalent of bird-watching. Every dive logbook has space to enter what you've seen on each dive, and learning to identify critters and noting them in your logbook becomes scuba's equivalent of the birder's life list. Because most marine

FIVE TIPS TO TUNE UP YOUR SKILLS

Writing in *Alert Diver,* Bill Clendenen, first training coordinator and then vice president of training for DAN, made five recommendations for divers who wanted to embark on scuba's equivalent to "self-help."

1. **Dive, Dive, Dive!** "Join a club, take a vacation, just do it," he wrote. "There's no better way to improve your diving than by diving regularly. By doing so, you keep your skills fresh. Diving requires motor skills which, when repeated on a regular basis, become familiar and comfortable. Unless you dive a couple of times a month, your buoyancy skills, buddy skills, and diving fitness are not likely to improve." He suggested joining a scuba club (a great way to hook up with dive buddies) and/or booking a dive trip (remember to sign up for a refresher course before you go).

2. **Buoyancy Control.** This he called "the art of 3-D movement with proper weighting and breathing." It's "one of the most difficult but important skills to master," and although it's one of the first skills learned in an introductory dive course, it's also one of the first to be forgotten. Do a *buoyancy check*, a surface skill that you practice in your confined- and open-water sessions. This is how it goes: Get into the water, fully weighted, equipped, and your air turned on. When you release the air from your BC and inhale, you should be floating eye-level with the water; when you exhale, you should sink slightly. If this occurs, you're neutrally buoyant. When you're underwater, practice breath control to adjust your position and streamline yourself. As you hone your buoyancy skills, you will probably be able to get by with less weight, thereby lessening fatigue.

3. **Get Back to Basics.** Because only instructors and their assistants regularly practice the basic skills, it's easy to get rusty. Resort-based instructors and dive guides commonly complain that vacationers aren't current with the basics. Many good resort dive operators now conduct a skills test, as well as look at new arrivals' C-cards and logbooks. Clendenen suggests that you ask yourself whether you're comfortable with your skills and your ability to conduct all phases of your dive plan. If not, taking a refresher course, practicing skills underwater, and boning up on theory are wise. "The purpose of a pool session is to regain comfort with your ability to perform your diving skills," he counseled.

4. **Snorkel Your Way to Fitness.** Snorkeling, discussed in chapter 8 (page 122), really is fundamental to diving and can help you become a better diver. "Many divers dismiss snorkeling as an activity that is better left to those unwilling to don tanks and regulators, but snorkeling is an underrated activity," Clendenen wrote. "Snorkeling provides additional opportunities to explore the undersea environment. Plus, it's one of the best ways to get yourself physically fit to dive."

5. **Know When to Say When.** This is Clendenen's way of reminding you to know your limits; if there's one sage piece of advice for new divers, heady from the accomplishment of certification, this is it. "The most common cause of diving accidents is 'diver error'—you, the diver, make a mistake," he wrote. "Whether it's a failure to maintain buddy contact or to frequently monitor time, depth, and air supply, injured divers sometimes exceed their limits." Here are the questions to ask yourself to determine whether a planned dive is—figuratively and literally—over your head: "Have I been trained to conduct this type of dive? Are the conditions similar to those that I have experienced? Is my buddy capable of conducting this dive? How am I feeling? Is my equipment functioning properly for me to do this dive?" He also stressed the importance of trusting your feelings about whether a planned dive is in your comfort zone.

—By Bill Clendenen, reproduced with permission from Divers Alert Network, *Alert Diver* (Sept./Oct. 1999)

"To me, scuba diving is 'feminine.' It's like going into a beautiful garden. It's all about ecology and feeling gentleness."

—Martha Slonim, Colorado Springs, Colorado

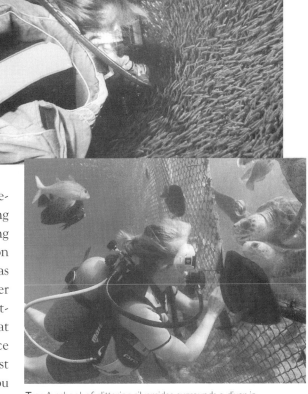

animals have no counterpart on land, divers wonder at the appearance and behavior of the critters in the sea.

Not long after you begin diving, your eyes will be drawn to fish charts posted on dive-shop or resort walls, and you will start buying waterproof fish-identification cards and studying fish books. You may sign up for a fish-identification course at a resort. You will probably discover, as many divers do, that the scenery is often better on a shallow dive than on a deep one. Color saturation is deeper (reds and yellows are lost at depth), sunlight filters through the water surface (which can be a comfort to new divers), and best of all, as you remember from your dive tables, you can stay underwater longer on shallower dives.

Top: A school of glittering silversides surrounds a diver in Cozumel. **Above:** Sea turtles snap up a free meal in Curaçao.

Although feeding wild animals is discouraged on land because it habituates them to human handouts, this isn't the case underwater. You shouldn't touch marine animals, but there's no harm in feeding fish—as long as you don't use one species to feed another. Dive guides sometimes use chunks of raw fish to attract barracudas or moray eels, but that's for them to do and not for us. Frozen peas are a popular fish food and local dive instructors and guides can advise you on what else to bring if you want to feed the fish.

Underwater photography and videography

Those who love to look at subaquatic creatures often want to capture them too. For snorkeling or shallow dives, you can buy an inexpensive, waterproof, disposable camera. However, once you get hooked on underwater photography, you may lust after an automatic dive camera, a waterproof housing for your 35-mm camera or, better yet, a submersible, 35-mm single-lens reflex camera, with specialty lenses, a strobe, or perhaps an underwater video setup.

Top left: Sophisticated underwater 35-mm camera and strobe. **Left:** Easy-to-use automatic dive camera. **Above:** Brilliant reef formations that are healthy and teeming with undersea life make for spectacular photographs.

Some divers begin photographing as an adjunct to their diving and some nature photographers get certified as an adjunct to their profession. Regardless of which is the cart and which is the seahorse, these two skills go well together. Resort-based dive operators often have loaner underwater cameras that guests may test, and some dive clubs have photo setups for their members to use. Liveaboards offer film processing. You also can take an underwater-photography specialty course and enter underwater-photo contests.

Reef diving

For many divers, the opportunity to explore reefs and the critters that dwell there epitomizes the sport's singular beauty. Built over time by small, simple, maritime animals, reefs develop into a rainbow of colors and an infinity of shapes. In addition to the sheer beauty, reefs are usually comfortable for new divers and even snorkelers. Many of the best sites are at 30 to 75 feet, kissed by the sun that filters down through the water. The colors are brilliant, the waters are often calm, and the splendor is unsurpassed.

Kelp diving

Diving amid the swaying "forests" of huge underwater plants called *kelp* is a specialty of West Coast diving. Teaming up with someone with strong underwater-compass skills is a must for anyone inexperienced in this wondrous environment. Kelp diving is considered cold-water diving—even if it's off the coast of southern California—so you'll need a thick wetsuit, gloves, and a dive hood. In some cases, the surface growth is so thick that diving under it can feel like diving in an overhead environment. It's possible to become entangled in the kelp, especially near the surface, so always carry a knife when kelp diving.

Night diving

A single reef looks and feels like a totally different environment at night, when nocturnal critters come out of hiding in search of food and when phosphorescent species add a particular supernatural element to the dive experience. Most dive destinations include at least one night dive each week on their roster. Buy or rent a dive light, make sure the battery is strong, attach a Cyalume glowstick to your tanks so you can be seen by dive pros and boat crews, and get set for a magical experience. Because night diving is not technically difficult and is usually done at a shallow dive site, it requires no special training if you follow an instructor, divemaster, or guide. If you go out on your own, however, you should have good underwater navigation skills.

Wall diving

In tropical waters, coral reefs often form right on the edge of the continental shelf. The landward side of the reef is usually a gentle sea bottom at comfortable diving depths, while the seaward side is a sheer underwater cliff that drops hundreds, even thousands, of feet to the seafloor. Diving along such a sheer cliff, known as a *wall*, is beautiful and thrilling. Sponges, sea fans, and soft coral grow abundantly from the wall, providing excellent habitat for small reef fish, which in turn draw the deep-water *pelagic* species. Wall dives are challenging because they take place at the edge of the open sea, where currents and surge must be considered.

"In my first 100 hours of diving, I never took my eyes off the reef wall. Then, on a trip to the Turks and Caicos in the Caribbean, a stranger pointed to something behind me— a humpback whale. It breached and came back down. That was the last time I went underwater without a camera. I've been to California to see mako and blue sharks, to Costa Rica and the Galapagos to dive with hammerheads, and to Thailand to see whale sharks. After diving both in cages and not, I know I actually feel safer in the open."

—Mary Peachin, Tucson, Arizona

TECHNICAL DIVING

"Tech diving was taboo when I first started. Often, in a class, I was told I was the first woman to do something. But I never felt a gender barrier. If anything, being a woman opened doors for me." So reported Jill Heinerth, interviewed in *Rodale's Scuba Diving*, following her record-setting 10,000-foot penetration of in the Wakulla Cave System of Florida. Her extraordinary effort included 11 hours of diving and 10 hours of decompression. Clearly, such feats are not for tyros.

Top: Underwater wreck exploration is like time travel beneath the sea. The quiet hulks of once-proud vessels are now part of the sub-aquatic environment. Wreck diving is a way to speculate on the ship's past. **Above:** Overhead environments, including caverns and wreck penetrations, require skill, experience, and training beyond the basics.

Wreck diving

Shipwrecks provide some of the most thrilling diving adventures. The popularity of the movie *Titanic* and the almost concurrent penetration of the real wreck by a deep-water submersible captured much attention. Scuba divers and even snorkelers can explore real wrecks of sunken ships, as well as airplanes and even ancient cities now beneath the water's surface. Whether they went under during pirate days on the Spanish Main, the fierce battles of World War II in the South Pacific, or a storm, sunken ships are interesting in and of themselves. Because they've become part of the undersea environment, they combine history, sometimes mystery, and breathtaking beauty. Plants and animals affix themselves to the wreck and fish are attracted to them.

Along with caves, lava tubes, and other natural features, wrecks fall into the general category of overhead environments because ceilings prevent divers from ascending straight up. Some natural wrecks, especially in popular dive destinations, have been cleaned up to remove the most blatant hazards to divers, such as sharp edges or spikes that can damage equipment. Decommissioned vessels also have been cleaned up and purposely sunk off shore to provide habitat for marine life, which divers can explore. The eastern coast of Florida, from Miami to Fort Lauderdale, is a noteworthy stretch where these so-called *artificial reefs* abound.

Some wrecks can be penetrated quite safely by new divers, especially when following a guide familiar with the layout. Others are complicated, with confusing labyrinths, dead ends, and passageways that slope down and lead deeper than the dive plan allows. Specialty classes train divers for the unique situations of *wreck diving*. If you or your buddy is claustrophobic or just cautious, you can taste the excitement by swimming around the outside of the wreck.

Ice diving

Die-hard divers in northern climates chop holes in lake ice and dive in the crystal-clear waters beneath it. To go ice diving, you need a fully accessorized dry suit, a special cold-water regulator, and other equipment, as well as a passion to breathe compressed air, no matter what. High-adventure diving is also done by technical divers in the Arctic and Antarctic regions.

Cave diving

With the exception of guided dives in select places (notably Mexico's Yucatán Peninsula), the high level of technical skill and special safety precautions required in natural overhead environments put cave diving in the realm of extremely advanced diving. It is dangerous and should not be attempted without specialized training.

Free diving

Free diving, an activity that predates recreational scuba diving, is regaining popularity. Here, a snorkeler free-dives with a bottlenose dolphin in the Bahamas.

An advanced specialty so old that it's new again, *free diving* is accomplished without a life-support system and on a single breath. This is the way the pre-scuba goggle divers of the 1930s did it—and the way sponge divers, pearl divers, and spearfishers did it in the past. Many snorkelers occasionally take a skin dive, holding their breath, kicking down to a shallow reef, and coming right up again. Free diving takes this skill and refines it. The main lure for recreational divers is the freedom from encumbering scuba gear. Snorkeling equipment, lungs, and nerve are required for free diving. New courses and certification begin with snorkeling skills, followed by an open-water certification for a breath-holding dive to 10 meters (33 feet).

At the highest level of skill, free divers use weights to descend, backed up by safety divers hanging onto a rope in case of emergency. In 1996, 18-year-old Mehgan Heany-Grier set the first U.S. record by diving to 155 feet and surfacing on a single breath of air. The following year, she topped her record by 10 feet. "I don't fear the ocean, but I have great respect for it," she says. "I don't drink, I don't do drugs, and I don't smoke. My adventure is the ocean, and that is what I want to do. There is nothing like the squeeze of the deep blue."

PADI and other organizations specialize in entry-level certification, recreational diving specialties, and instructor certification in their systems and progression, but other organizations focus on advanced diving only (see chapter 10, Resources). For example, American Nitrox Divers International was founded to establish standards and procedures for cutting-edge technologies and diving. Their branded enriched-air product is called SafeAir, and they offer training for SafeAir divers from recreational use to technical and extended-range diving, as well as more exotic gas mixes and rebreather training—and of course, training for instructors at all levels.

WATER WORLD

Water is wet, but that's not all. Water can be fresh or saline (salty); still or flowing; confined in a pool, a flooded quarry, or a lake; or open to wave, wind, and tidal action. For divers, the basic categories are warm or cold, salt or fresh. Most people consider warm salt water the most benign dive environment. When divers travel for their sport, it's usually to such places. In fact, nearly two thirds of all diving is now done in tropical waters—no matter where the divers actually live. What you wear to dive is determined by the temperature of the waters at your destination.

Salt water laps against America's long coastline and surrounds the world's islands. Freshwater diving can be done in lakes, old quarries, and even some rivers. Lake diving takes place in water ranging from ponds to the Great Lakes, which offer astonishing marine life and amazing wrecks. Obviously, river diving is concentrated in suitable portions of wide rivers—think Mississippi or Schuylkill—rather than fast-flowing flumes with whitewater, rapids, and rocks. Unless you're a freshwater diver who stays in local lakes or quarries, your experience and knowledge will eventually include ocean factors such as wave action, tides, and current.

As a resort diver or as a newly certified diver, you will probably have an easier time than I did on my first aborted 90-foot checkout dive (see pages 65–66). You will most likely begin your open-water dive career descending to depths ranging from 40 to 60 feet. Beyond that, training and experience are useful. When 80 or 100 feet of even the clearest sea is between you and the sky, you're in a blue world; the water filters out reds and yellows. Once you're certified and on a dive boat, 90 to 100 feet on the first dive of the day is not unusual. As you get some more experience, you might go down to 130 feet, perhaps diving along the edge of the underwater wall of a coastal shelf or to a wreck. At these depths, the water filters out most colors of the spectrum, and your environment is deep blue.

When water temperatures are near freezing, it's possible to dive only if wearing a dry suit.

MORE ON WHAT TO WEAR
• • • • • • • • • • • • • • • • • • • •

Warm water is between the mid-70s and mid-80s°F, which is normally comfortable in a dive skin or a shortie wetsuit. Warm-blooded divers sometimes find that simply a T-shirt over a bathing suit is enough. Some sheltered tropical waters are in the mid-80s, in which a swimsuit suffices. Cold water refers to a far greater range, from the mid-70s all the way down to near freezing. On the high end of the cold-water scale, you need a light wetsuit. As the water temperature drops, you need a heavier wetsuit and probably gloves and a dive hood. In still colder water, a very thick wetsuit is required to avoid hypothermia, and in the coldest waters and for ice diving, a dry suit is mandatory (this is specialty diving that uses skills and knowledge beyond the entry level). When planning a single dive, conditions such as very cold water or high altitude must be factored in.

For more on exposure protection, see pages 42–44.

TAKING CERTIFICATION TO A HIGHER LEVEL

Every certifying agency has its own names for each level of scuba proficiency that it offers, and not all offer every level. Some specialize in entry-level diving, others in advanced or technical diving, and some offer a wide range of courses. Because it's the biggest mainstream organization, I include the following list of PADI courses and certifications beyond the basics to show you the paths to follow to become an advanced or even professional diver.

A C-card is like a learner's permit for divers: it allows you to begin learning about diving firsthand.

Specialty diver

To progress from the basic Open-Water Diver level and become an Advanced Open-Water Diver under the PADI system, you must demonstrate five in-water skills from the following list of specialties. To gain Advanced Plus certification, you must do nine of them, and to be a Master Scuba Diver you must have reached that level and also complete a Rescue Diver Course (below).

- altitude diver
- deep diver
- drift diver
- dry-suit diver
- *multilevel diver*
- peak performance buoyancy
- underwater naturalist
- underwater photographer
- Project AWARE fish identification (see page 107)
- dive propulsion vehicle
- night diver
- search-and-recovery diver
- underwater videographer
- underwater navigator
- wreck diver

Diving in Arctic or Antarctic waters is the epitome of cold-water diving, most often the province of marine biologists and other scientists, and a few of the most adventurous and highly trained recreational divers. Special equipment is also necessary to dive in such extreme conditions.

If you're already an Advanced Open-Water Diver and wish to continue your skill building, you can take any of the skills tests above, beyond your original five, and are also eligible for the following.

- cavern diver
- deep diver (higher level)
- enriched-air diver
- ice diver
- wreck diver (higher level)

If the safety element of diving and the ability to respond to emergency situations appeals to you—or if, as it is for many, it is the next step toward really advanced diving—PADI offers medic first-aid training for divers and non-divers. With that training, you can proceed to becoming a rescue diver. Beyond that, the track transitions from recreational to professional. The courses are

- dive master
- assistant instructor
- instructor
- specialty instructor
- medic first-aid instructor
- master scuba dive trainer
- course director

PASSING THE TORCH

No matter when, how, or why they start, some women become so enamored of it that it turns into their livelihood. One woman who felt such a calling is Anne Sadovsky Koepf of Healdsburg, California. Growing up in a family where the bar of achievement was set high, she nevertheless spent many years assuming that diving was not for her, but when she tried it, she was bitten hard by the scuba bug. "I came from a long line of super-jocks. My dad played three sports while in medical school and made it to the Olympic trials for long-distance swimming," she says. "Some of his times haven't been repeated in almost 70 years. I'm the oldest of six children, all a year apart. We swam and skied competitively growing up in Michigan, but I never felt 'good enough' at many things. My brothers became certified to dive in Michigan, and both my sisters became divers, but I always felt I wasn't 'good enough,' so I never tried. Then, three years ago, a woman colleague who was in her late 50s said she was taking up diving. I thought, 'If she can, maybe I can, too.' My dad, still alive at 87, said, 'Anne, of course you can do it. You're very comfortable in the water.' And I did. Now I'm an independent instructor affiliated with two dive centers in California and one in Mexico." Women as enthusiastic as Anne pass their passion on to the new divers they teach.

DIVING FOR CREDIT

The American Council on Education has established college or university credits in recreation and/or physical education for certain PADI courses, whether or not the courses are actually conducted at or by the school. If the courses are held off-campus, PADI will send transcripts that colleges normally honor as they would transfer credits from another institution. PADI courses and their recommended credits are as shown above.

You may decide to become proficient in one or more specialties just to enhance your own diving or, if the lure of the sea is great, advanced certification levels may lead to an underwater career.

DIVING FOR DOLLARS

When you read all the complexities involved in diving and the cautions that diving requires every time you go under, you may be tempted to bag the whole idea. However, the most powerful proof of scuba diving's seductiveness is in the thousands of people—including many women in most specialties—who have made diving their career.

Dive instructor

Because certifying agencies offer an easy progression of steps from the first C-card to advanced levels, working toward instructor certification is a natural for anyone who loves to dive. Good interpersonal skills and patience for teaching beginners are real pluses for anyone thinking of becoming a dive instructor. You don't need to move to an exotic locale to teach diving. You can work at a local dive shop, where evening and weekend opportunities abound. In addition to

"I was born in New Jersey and moved to Florida when I was 12. The ocean was my backyard."

—Dr. Sylvia Earle, marine biologist, author, and National Geographic Society Explorer-in-Residence

College Credits

Course	Credits
Open-Water Diver	1
Advanced Open-Water Diver	1
Advanced Plus	1
Night Diver	1
Deep Diver	1
Rescue Diver	1
Divemaster	2
Instructor Development	2
Course Director Training	3

Sue Smith of the Shark Research Institute tags a whale shark. She is skin diving rather than using bulky scuba gear.

● ●

"**A** long time ago, I was surface swimming on Lake Erie. I swam over *The Prince*, a wreck in 15 feet of water. I looked down and I could see it! Just seeing something underwater, I was hooked. I wanted to take a scuba course. My husband didn't dive, so I thought if I wanted to stay current in my dive skills, I'd help the instructor. I thought, 'I can teach better than this guy.' So I became an instructor. I love to teach people skills they didn't know. I've seen scuba change lives."

—Ellen Holland Keller, YMCA Scuba, Cleveland, Ohio

● ●

teaching in a classroom and pool, with occasional diving, you may be asked to work on a shop's retail sales floor or at a resort operation's beach booth. You won't always have to teach beginners if you continue your training to also teach specialty classes.

Marine biologist

This is one of the glamour tracks that involve diving. Dr. Sylvia Earle, a preeminent marine biologist, is arguably the best-known diver whose last name is not Cousteau. Marine biologists spend time in the lab, of course, but their fieldwork takes place underwater. A scientific bent, a willingness to work toward an advanced degree, and a penchant for environmental issues help spawn a successful career. Maritime institutes, environmental organizations, universities, aquariums, and government agencies are some of the institutions that employ marine biologists.

Left: Marine biologists get to play in environments such as the Kelp Forest in the Monterey Bay Aquarium. **Above:** Underwater photographer training her camera on a lionfish—venomous to touch but spectacular to photograph.

Underwater naturalist or archaeologist

Combining knowledge of marine life with the skills of a park ranger, naturalists work at marine sanctuaries and underwater parks. They conduct topside classes on fish identification, lead snorkelers and divers on naturalist tours, and conduct fish counts. The Virgin Islands National Park, on St. John, is the most famous park that employs underwater naturalists.

Karen Kozlowski, a marine archaeologist with the Monitor National Marine Sanctuary, worked with 40 navy deep-sea divers who excavated and explored the famous Civil War ironclad. The National Park Service's Submerged Cultural Resources Unit deploys underwater archaeologists, cartographers, and technicians of various types to map, manage, and preserve shipwrecks in its waters, and international teams of dive professionals with similar expertise explore, document, and retrieve or preserve such underwater artifacts as sunken cities and shipwrecks around the world from Alexandria to Zanzibar too. Verlora Peacock, for instance, was the only woman on a 10-diver team that spent three months in the South Pacific, recovering the remains of *Nuestra Señora de Pilar*, a Spanish galleon that sank in 1690. Heady stuff for an archaeologist—or anyone who wants to combine passions for history and diving.

Dive journalist or photographer

For those who have a way with words or a golden eye, communicating the wonders of the underwater world can become a career. Dive publications need editors, writers, photographers, and equipment-testers. Nondive publications occasionally run dive articles as well, whose words and pictures come from divers. Dive equipment catalogs, calendar publishers, and advertising

Marine attractions and aquariums need divers to interact with the animals and do other paid and volunteer jobs. This diver feeds sharks at Curaçao's Animal Adventures.

• •

"**D**iving changed my life. I learned to dive 20 years ago. Then I picked up a camera and started working for a fishing magazine. I wrote a lobster guide called *Get More Tail*, and started getting letters from indignant women. It's been interesting. I've dived in many places, and had photographs and articles published. I wouldn't be a writer or a photographer without diving."

—Linda Reeves, Delray Beach, Florida

• •

Aquarium worker

agencies often assign photographers or buy stock photos from them. The queen of dive journalists is Bonnie Cardone, who started working for *Skin Diver* magazine in 1976 and became its editor 21 years later.

Dive supplier employee

Manufacturers of dive equipment and clothing employ the same range of talents as any other business that sells a product. Whatever your business or creative talents may be, there is a job for you with a supplier: accountant, designer, sales and marketing specialist, business manager— even a shipping clerk can find a slot with a dive purveyor.

One—and only one—university in the world offers a four-year degree program in Sport Management with a track in the Dive Industry. Barry University in Miami Shores has a SM/DI program in the School of Human Performance and Leisure Sciences that leads to a bachelor's degree. The school's core courses include fundamentals of the human body, sport, and movement science. SM/DI majors also study accounting, computer applications, retailing, advertising, marketing, and managerial skills, and are offered a full-time internship during senior year. (See chapter 10, Resources, for contact information.)

If blowing bubbles and swimming with the fish appeal to you but an exotic location does not, there may be a spot in an aquarium. There are about 50 aquariums in the United States, with another 20 under construction or planned. Divers feed fish, tend real and fake underwater plants, and clean the acrylic that separates the critters from the public.

Search-and-rescue diver

Police and sheriff's departments and other investigative agencies use divers to search and retrieve objects—yes, sometimes bodies—from the water, often in low visibility or turbulent seas. These divers make the news when an airplane crashes in the ocean or a river and they are sent in to look for the voice and flight data recorders—and anything else that might reveal the cause of the accident. If law enforcement appeals to you, it combines well with diving in some parts of the country.

Military diver

From the early Frogmen to the famous Seals, whose training is among the most rigorous of any branch of the military, these divers comprise the U.S. Navy's corps of divers. Military diving is traditionally a man's world because of its combat potential, but the services are opening an increasing number of doors to women. Ask a recruiter if you're interested.

Commercial diver

Underwater welding and other jobs required on oil rigs, bridges, and other structures are not traditional women's work either. But if it's appealing to you, training and jobs are available.

VOLUNTEER OPPORTUNITIES

Beach and underwater cleanups, fish counts, and underwater pollution monitoring are just a few of the volunteer opportunities for divers to give something back to their sport. If you live near the water, check with your local dive operator to see how you can help.

On the third Saturday in September, more than a half-million volunteers worldwide participate in the Project AWARE (Aquatic World Awareness, Responsibility, and Education) annual International Coastal Cleanup Day (see chapter 10, Resources, for contact information on how to participate in or organize a cleanup). It's the largest volunteer effort on earth on behalf of the aquatic environment. In 1999, 900 underwater and beach sites around the world were cleaned of trash.

During the first two weeks in July, volunteer divers and snorkelers participate in the Great American Fish Count to raise awareness of and provide information about fish populations. Participants attend free seminars in visual fish identification—a helpful skill for recreational diving, as well as a benefit to the subaquatic environment. The island of Bonaire, a popular dive destination in the Netherlands Antilles, hosts the annual Bonaire Dive Festival during the first half of November. It features conservation diving in Bonaire Marine Park, experts in the marine environment and underwater photography, and great socializing. For details on these and other volunteer programs, contact the environmental organizations listed in chapter 10, Resources.

Chapter 8

THE SOFTER SIDE OF SCUBA

Whenever you're underwater, enraptured by the beautiful and often benign undersea environment, you sense that scuba diving is the most feminine of sports. When you watch the abundant sea life—marine mammals with their young; schools of fish; underwater plants and simple animal organisms establishing themselves on rocks, walls, and wrecks; or turtles swimming determinedly toward their breeding grounds—the subaquatic realm presents an intensely female side. This feeling overwhelms many women divers, who become figuratively and literally immersed in the world beneath the sea's surface.

This feeling washes away the nuts-and-bolts issues of equipment, the brain-draining calculations of dive tables, the tedium of the classroom when you were eager to get underwater, and the pit-of-the-stomach nervousness that preceded your open-water dives. There's beauty and magic underwater, and most women want to share it. Fortunately, the dive boat, the buddy system, and the easy sociability after diving foster such camaraderie, especially in a resort setting or when diving locally with friends or family.

THE UNDERSEA ENVIRONMENT

More than 70 percent of the earth (i.e., 80 percent of the Southern Hemisphere, 61 percent of the Northern Hemisphere) is covered by ocean. No one knows exactly how many species live beneath the seas. In fact, new ones are still being discovered and a species believed to be extinct occasionally is found in some distant corner of the globe. The best guess is that there are approximately 1.5 million types of living organisms—plants and animals—on earth today. Of those, tens of thousands are marine species that live in saltwater and freshwater environments, including the following:

- as many as 24,000 varieties of microscopic plant forms such as algae, diatoms, and dinoflagellates

- 30,000 single-celled animals called protozoa

- 10,000 species of sponge

- 10,000 types of coral, hydroid, jellyfish, and sea anemone

- 44,000 species of underwater worms

- 30,000 crustaceans, including crab, lobster, shrimp, and microscopic plankton

- 75,000 mollusks, including abalone, chiton, clams, cuttlefish, limpets, mussels, nautilus, oysters, octopus, scallops, sea slugs, shrimp, and squid

- as many as 5,000 moss animals

- 5,900 basket stars, brittle stars, feather stars, sea cucumbers, sand dollars, sea lilies, sea stars, and sea urchins

- 1,350 chordates, which represent a biological link between vertebrate and invertebrate species

- 19,000 fish species

- 6,000 reptiles, including marine iguanas, sea turtles, and sea snakes

- hundreds of marine mammals, including dolphins, manatees, sea otters, sea lions, seals, walruses, and whales

• •

"In Tobago, I had my first encounter with a manta ray. My heart melted as she—her eyes were much too soft to be a male's—emerged from the depths, circled our group, and glided along beside me for a while, curious at such a clumsy creature in her environment. Every encounter with the big pelagics is not unlike meeting an alien from another planet. Who needs to go into outer space when we have a world under the sea we've barely explored?"

—Dale Leatherman, Snowshoe, West Virginia

• •

Top: A curious stingray comes along to make friends with this diver. **Above:** Healthy reefs, clean waters, and controlled fishing result in an abundance of marine animals.

Mammals and large or colorful fish tend to capture our attention and imagination (remember *Free Willy?*), but the building blocks of healthy oceans—and a healthy planet—rest in the less glamorous (often invisible, creepy, or dangerous) creatures. There's nothing like diving to bring out the environmentalist in a woman. Several years ago, I dived Honduras's splendid protected reef area off the island of Roatán. The fish were astonishing, the corals were brilliant, and the seafloor was as clean as a Dutch kitchen. The fish population appeared healthy even though locals were permitted to use fishing lines and hooks, even in the marine sanctuary. Six months later, I dived the same reef, near a small island called Upper Utila, on which a fishing village is located. Villagers toss their trash on the beach, and the few small fish that remain seek refuge amid the battered coral. Upper Utilans have overfished their waters, beyond the level of sustainability.

Upper Utila is a microcosm of what has happened to a tragic number of the world's oceans, bays, lakes, and rivers, which once teemed with aquatic life. The litany of what we have done—or have allowed to be done—to the world's waters is sickening. Factory trawlers scoop up in their nets anything that swims in the sea, killing or damaging whatever isn't processed. Norway's whalers are dispatched by an otherwise peaceable country that refuses to sign an international treaty against whaling. Shark-finning is a horrific practice in which the fins of captured sharks are removed to supply the key ingredient for a Chinese delicacy called *shark-fin soup*; the bleeding animals are tossed back into the sea to die. Sword-fishing boats trail lines with baited hooks for up to 40 miles. Paradise Reef off Cozumel, Mexico, was destroyed to build a pier so that cruise-ship passengers could disembark directly, instead of being ferried ashore by tenders. Industrial pollutants, fertilizers and pesticides, refuse, and human wastes are dumped into the water all over the world. Considering all the abuse, it's a wonder that there's any life at all left in the earth's waters.

Once you become a diver, you may pay more attention to these issues by contributing to marine environmental causes, writing letters to your senators and representatives, and volunteering for maritime and shore cleanup projects. Saving our waters and allowing them to recuperate, before it's too late, is a big job. Divers are on the forefront of cleaning up coastal waters and coastlines, hoping that their efforts will help the seas recover as well. Marine environmental organizations are listed in chapter 10, Resources.

RESPONSIBLE DIVING—AND DINING

When you've had the thrill of seeing marine life in its natural environment, you might find yourself wondering how your eating habits are impacting it. Dr. Sylvia Earle explains the connection between "fish" and "seafood" with succinct logic. "Divers see firsthand that the sea is alive with small, medium, and very large creatures that are as curious about us as we are about them," she writes. "We get to know individual fish swimming in a blue ocean, not just swimming in lemon slices and butter."

If you delve into seafood-gathering practices, you might adjust what you eat. Some of this awareness has already impacted the marketplace. For example, many people purchase canned tuna that has been caught only in dolphin-safe nets, following public outrage about how dolphins were caught as "bycatch" (the fishing industry's term for impact on other species) of tuna harvesting (see below). Other fish production practices are less well known. Orange roughy, for instance, is a deep-water fish taken from the seafloor by literally churning everything up, killing other creatures and destroying habitat in the process. Even raised species are no guarantee of environmental responsibility. Jumbo shrimp from places like Ecuador and Thailand are raised in con-

● ●

Seafood Watch

Best Choices	Potential Problems	Avoid
calamari/squid	clams (farmed)	Atlantic cod
catfish (farmed)	imitation crab/surimi/pollock	lingcod
New Zealand cod/hoki	snow crab	American lobster
Alaskan halibut	Pacific/California halibut	monkfish
Dungeness crab	mussels (farmed)	orange roughy
mahi-mahi/dolphinfish/dorado	oysters (farmed)	rockfish/Pacific red snapper/rock cod
Alaska salmon (wild-caught)	Pacific Coast salmon (wild-caught)	sablefish/butterfish/black cod
striped bass (farmed)	bay scallops	Atlantic sea scallops
sturgeon (farmed)	bay shrimp/Pacific pink shrimp	Chilean seabass/Patagonian toothfish
tilapia (farmed)	spot prawns (trap-caught only)	shark (all)
rainbow trout (farmed)	Turtle-Safe shrimp/prawns	spot prawns (trawl-caught)
	English/petrale sole	prawns (wild-caught or farmed)
	Albacore tuna	swordfish
	yellowfin tuna/ahi (Hawaiian line-caught)	bluefin tuna

● ●

NATIONAL MARINE SANCTUARIES

• • • • • • • • • • • • • • • •

The National Oceanic and Atmospheric Administration (NOAA) has designated a dozen marine sanctuaries, totaling approximately 18,000 square miles, to protect their natural and historical legacy. These sanctuaries are based on our national-park model. Dr. Sylvia Earle called them "special places [that] represent hope for troubled waters and the species that live in them." They offer some of America's most pristine diving. For a list, see chapter 10, Resources.

A diver peers through sea fans and coral, common features in tropical waters.

crete tanks, typically in mangrove areas. Mangroves are considered by many to be the "nursery of the seas" because so many fish spawn there. Yet when the tanks are rinsed out, the powerful residue from shrimp farming kills the marine life and eventually the mangroves too.

If you care enough about the health of the planet's oceans to do your part with every forkful, check out *Audubon Magazine*'s rating of seafood by the size and viability of the fish population, as well as bycatch. (The dolphin and orange-roughy issues are examples of bycatch problems.)

Aquariums, marine-life institutions, and even environmentally conscious natural-foods markets post or distribute a condensed version of *Audubon*'s list called Seafood Watch (see previous page), which guides conscientious consumers about seafood purchases in regard to species health, sustainability, and harvesting practices. Some are real eye-openers.

Where to dive

You can dive virtually anywhere there is water. Seacoasts, slow-moving rivers, lakes, reservoirs, and flooded quarries all lure divers who grasp any opportunity to breathe compressed air. There are lots of wonders down under. The New Jersey coast is famous for shipwrecks. Catalina Island, off the California coast, is famous for its magical kelp forests. Puget Sound, way up in Washington State, has world-class octopus on display for visiting divers. Fort Lauderdale, just north of what are considered tropical waters, has the best artificial reef system on the East Coast. Some areas are naturally remote and diving is a solitary pleasure. Other areas have been set aside for marine conservation. At still others, divers hope that ship captains, harbor pilots, and pleasure-boat owners pay attention to the red and white dive flags that mark their dive sites.

Elsewhere in the world, an additional 1,200 areas have some level of official protection, including Australia's Great Barrier Reef, Bonaire's Marine Park, and Roatán, off the coast of Honduras.

DREAM DIVE TRIPS

Some people travel to dive, others dive to travel. The destinations include some of the most beautiful and exotic places on earth. Although it's possible to plan an interesting and successful dive trip to northern areas, most vacationers prefer tropical or warm-water diving—and dive stores in northerly climates regularly organize dive trips to warm-water, warm-weather destinations. For these trips, you buy an air-land package vacation, which includes transportation, lodging, usually some meals, and diving. In addition, you travel with personnel from your own dive shop (perhaps even the instructor who certified you); local guides or instructors usually accompany the group on the dives. If your dive shop's schedule does not match yours, consult with the in-house travel agency that many shops operate; the agent is likely to be knowledgeable about dive destinations. Dive magazines are also full of ads for great trips, and you'll also find some leading operators in chapter 10, Resources.

Dive vacations fall into three basic categories, and each has benefits and drawbacks.

Resorts: Designed for diving (or diving as a bonus)

There are dedicated dive resorts where virtually everyone dives (those few spouses or companions who don't dive at least snorkel). Such a resort's own dive boats are usually tied up to a dock right on the premises. These resorts are excellent for both

UNDERSEA ENCOUNTERS

• • • • • • • • • • • • • • • • • • •

"I got certified in the Maldive Islands in the Pacific. When my classmates and I resurfaced after each dive, they would talk about how exhilarating it was, how amazing. As soon as I realized that my fear was preventing me from enjoying anything, the fear disappeared. With my new confidence I found out what my classmates had already discovered: diving is incredible. On my last dive, I fearlessly watched white-tip reef sharks and was mesmerized by turtles making their way up the bank to the reefs. I giggled at the looks of the clownfish. I felt tickled yellow and blue as I swam through a school of royal fusiliers. When an 18-foot manta ray hovered overhead, I felt as if I were in an episode of *Close Encounters of the Underwater Kind*. Now I am a diver. I say it confidently —and probably a bit too often."

—Amy Richards, New York

hard-core and enthusiastic novice divers: they tend to have a laid-back and congenial atmosphere, and the talk around the bar in the evening revolves around diving. They are appropriate for nondiving companions as well because other resort activities are usually available.

Other tropical resorts have affiliated and convenient on-site dive operations, but diving is just one of many options. Whether the barefoot-casual style of the dive resorts or more formal, the dive ambiance at these resorts is diluted by golfers, sun-worshippers, spa aficionados, sea-kayakers, sightseers, shoppers, and other vacationers who believe that *their* sport or interest is the best. These resorts are excellent for families or groups with different interests, or might be a good choice if you're a new diver and not certain that you want to devote your entire trip to diving.

Club Med: A format that works

Club Med's dedicated dive centers merit a special mention because they are well suited for new divers, and they are also a good choice for a family or group of friends in which some dive and some don't. Club Med has its own scuba school, leading to a basic level of certification that is valid for diving at clubs all over the world, and it also accepts C-cards from all certifying agencies.

The club's dive boats are well set up and efficiently run, and the divemasters and instructors are generally well attuned to beginners. The usual format on dive programs is two morning dives each day, leaving the afternoon free for other Club Med activities. Club Med is a good choice for families because children's activities are organized six days a week and included in the package price.

Clubs that feature diving are Buccaneer's Creek, Martinique; Columbus Isle, The Bahamas; St. Lucia, West Indies; Sonora Bay, Mexico; Turkoise, Turks and Caicos, and Moorea in the South Pacific. (See chapter 10, Resources, for contact information.)

Diving à la Disney

Arguably the most programmed dive experience on the planet is Epcot DiveQuest, a feature of the Living Seas Pavilion at Florida's Walt Disney World. The diving is done in a 5.7-million-gallon saltwater aquarium, one of the world's largest, which is inhabited by 65 species, including up to 3,000 reef fish, huge turtles, eagle rays, and what Disney promises are "nonaggressive sharks."

After suiting up in waist-deep water, groups of eight divers follow a dive guide on a 20-minute underwater tour, followed by another 20 minutes of independent diving. Dives are currently scheduled daily at 4:30 and 5:30 P.M. You wouldn't think that a C-card would be necessary for an aquarium with a maximum depth of 27 feet, but it is.

All equipment plus a T-shirt, a certificate (signed by Mickey Minnow, perhaps?), and a logbook stamp are included in the $140 price (call 407-WDW-TOUR/407-939-8687 for reservations). And while Mom is diving, the kids can sample the park's other attractions.

Liveaboards: All diving, all the time

A *liveaboard* is a cabin cruiser outfitted for diving with accoutrements such as a dive platform on the stern and an onboard air compressor for filling tanks. Increasingly, liveaboards have onboard facilities for E6 film processing, a great benefit for dive photographers. Instructors, dive guides, or divemasters are part of the crew. A vacation on such a boat is the purest dive experience you can have. Because there are no daily cruises from a resort to dive sites, four or even five dives a day are not uncommon, and because the boats are relatively small (compared to a resort), groups are small too.

On a liveaboard, you sleep, eat, and participate in low-key evening activities, which seem to

Liveaboards provide the most intense dive vacation options. Treasured by experienced divers, they also give new divers a chance to get in a lot of diving and immerse themselves into the world of the aficionado 24 hours a day.

involve a great deal of dive talk. On some liveaboards, you dive directly off the boat; others act like a mother ship, from which small boats or inflatables set out to dive sites a short distance away. Most often, the boat concentrates on one general diving area a day and then travels overnight to another area. Some boats are part of a fleet; others are independently owned. Generally speaking, fleet boats are more luxurious—*luxury* being a relative term—than independents.

Liveaboards are like mini-cruise ships but with virtually no frills. Cabins are compact with either shared or private toilet facilities and may or may not be air-conditioned. There may also be a desalinization unit to provide ample fresh water for the entire trip, without rationing. If you tend to get seasick or claustrophobic, or you simply prefer variety when you're vacationing, a liveaboard won't be the right choice. People not passionate about diving may find the ambiance to be "live-a-bored." However, if you want to both literally and figuratively immerse yourself in diving, you won't find a better scuba vacation anywhere.

Dive towns: Variety and price

Towns that happen to be in the center of dive action can provide well-priced vacations and plenty to do when you're not underwater. Nondive sports, shopping, nightlife, and family activities abound in these places.

In the United States, Fort Lauderdale has become a top dive destination for mainland Florida for these reasons. Just offshore are numerous artificial reefs. The city offers ample accommodations, from budget motels and condominiums to luxury spa-resorts. Summer is prime dive season, which is off-season for general tourism and, therefore, a bargain, in the general scheme of things. Although September is the tail end of the season, its designation as Scuba Month of

TOP DIVE DESTINATIONS

Caribbean and Atlantic Islands
- Little Cayman
- Cozumel, Mexico
- Bonaire
- Belize
- Cayman Brac
- St. Croix, U.S. Virgin Islands
- Walker's Cay, Bahamas
- Saba
- Utila, Bay Islands, Honduras
- Grand Turk, Turks, and Caicos

North America
- Morehead City, North Carolina
- Tobermory, Ontario
- British Columbia
- Flower Garden Banks, Texas
- Key Largo, Florida
- Palm Beach County, Florida
- Tavernier, Florida
- Looe Key, Florida
- Islamorada, Florida
- Monterey, California

Indo-Pacific
- Galapagos Islands
- Palau, Micronesia
- Great Barrier Reef, Australia
- Red Sea, Egypt
- Island of Maui, Hawaii
- Island of Hawaii, Hawaii
- Papua New Guinea
- Oahu, Hawaii
- Fiji
- Costa Rica

Following are the readers' rankings of the best destinations for beginning divers.

Caribbean and Atlantic
- Bermuda
- Bonaire
- St. Thomas, U.S. Virgin Islands
- St. Croix, U.S. Virgin Islands
- British Virgin Islands

Greater Fort Lauderdale provides well-priced dive packages, special dive events, and even dive-oriented educational programs. In Mexico, Cozumel has a similar reputation. The island has many lodging properties and dive operators, which can be booked independently or combined into a dive package.

Based on over 600 responses in 1999–2000 to its annual survey, *Rodale's Scuba Diving* compiled a list of destinations that the magazine's readers and web users identified as the best overall dive destinations, starting with the most popular choices (see sidebar).

SELECTING A DIVE DESTINATION

When you decide to go on a dive trip, your destination may be selected for you if you go with your local dive shop, dive club (see page 118), or friends who have planned a trip. If you're the sole or prime decision-maker on where to travel, you will calculate such variables as price, type of destination

North America
- Looe Key, Florida
- Tavernier, Florida
- Key Largo, Florida
- Tobermory, Ontario
- Islamorada, Florida

Indo-Pacific
- Island of Hawaii, Hawaii
- Maui, Hawaii
- Oahu, Hawaii
- French Polynesia
- Yap, Micronesia

North America
- British Columbia
- Palm Beach County, Florida
- Flower Garden Banks, Texas
- Key Largo, Florida
- Tavernier, Florida

Indo-Pacific
- Red Sea, Egypt
- Galapagos Islands
- Great Barrier Reef, Australia
- Palau, Micronesia
- Truk Lagoon, Micronesia

*—Reprinted with permission from Rodale's
Scuba Diving (Jan./Feb. 2000)*

Rodale's readers selected the following as the best-value destinations.

Caribbean and Atlantic
- Utila, Bay Islands, Honduras
- Cozumel, Mexico
- Walker's Cay, Bahamas
- Bimini, Bahamas
- St. Croix, U.S. Virgin Islands

(dive resort, liveaboard, and so on), and convenience to where you live. However, you should also consider how the dive destination and the dive operator that you select treat the marine environment. The importance of protecting reefs and other fragile areas and not interfering in the health of underwater plant and animal species is where dive travel and marine ecology meet.

"**W**e took a family vacation to the Caribbean every year when our kids were small. While my husband played golf, I snorkeled with the kids. We all had the desire to get certified. Eventually, my children both became certified and so did I. They went away to college, and my husband and I continue to take Caribbean vacations. He still plays golf and I dive as much as I can."

—Carole Morris, Chicago, Illinois

TOP DIVE DESTINATIONS

• •

Here are a dozen destinations that are consistently rated tops for scuba diving. They are highly recommended for both novice and more advanced divers.

- Aruba
- Australia (Great Barrier Reef)
- Bahamas (specifically New Providence and Grand Bahama)
- Belize

- Bonaire
- Cayman Islands
- Cozumel
- Florida Keys
- French Polynesia (Bora Bora and Moorea)

- The Grenadines (notably Bequia and St. Lucia)
- Hawaii
- Honduras (specifically Roatán, but also other Bay Islands)

• •

"**A**lthough I had gotten certified while in college in New England and done my checkout dives in Long Island Sound, I didn't discover the joys of diving until 12 years later. I was in Honduras as the trip secretary on a trip for Interplast, an international volunteer medical organization that provides free reconstructive surgery for children in developing countries. Our team worked two long weeks in hot, humid San Pedro Sula, doing over 100 operations, and we were ready for adventure. Several of us flew the short hop to Roatán for the weekend. I was extremely nervous about diving, but after a thorough refresher course, I felt ready to jump into the sea. I was stunned by the beauty of the coral formations on the north side of Roatán, as well as the variety of fish. On my very first dive, we saw a nurse shark, some big barracuda, a leopard ray, and a moray. I've been back diving ever since."

—Amy Laden, Mountainview, California

The Coral Reef Alliance (see chapter 10, Resources) prepared the checklist in the sidebar on page 119 for the U.N. Conference on Sustainable Tourism and the International Coral Reef Initiative Workshop. These questions are ones that you can directly ask your local dive shop or a dive tour operator, as well as indirectly through them to resort owners, dive-boat operators, and others involved in dive tourism.

SCUBA DIVING CLUBS

For economy, socializing, and your best shot at local diving, join a scuba club. Some clubs have their own boats; others charter. It's a good way to hook up with a buddy. Your local dive center can provide contacts or you can check the Internet for a dive club located near you.

CORAL REEF ALLIANCE CHECKLIST FOR DIVE OPERATORS AND DIVERS

Checklist for Dive Destinations

- Are visitors encouraged to learn about the geography, culture, and ecology of dive destinations prior to leaving home?
- Is pre-trip information about the destination's local customs and proper diving etiquette provided to all visitors?
- Is specific attention drawn to coral reef ecology and to guidelines and regulations for boating, snorkeling, scuba diving, fishing, and other recreational uses of the reef?
- Are tours designed to enhance visitor awareness and understanding of the coral reef ecosystems that will be visited?

When Selecting a Dive Destination

- Are visitors encouraged to participate in local conservation efforts, particularly regarding the use of energy and fresh water?
- Are visitors informed of how they can make donations or give other support to local coral reef conservation initiatives?
- Do tour operators donate money or assistance to help the local environment?
- Is all construction and landscaping planned to avoid negative environmental impacts of visitors, particularly in protected marine areas?
- Is public participation sought and encouraged for all projects affecting the community?
- Are local traditions and use patterns for the reefs respected?
- Are local naturalists [and divemasters] hired when possible and appropriate?
- Do visitors stay in lodging that fits the environment?
- Are local businesses and service providers supported as much as possible?
- Are visitors encouraged to buy authentic arts and crafts from local artisans, and to purchase other products and services that benefit the local economy?

- Is purchasing coral or souvenirs made from coral, turtles, and other threatened wildlife prohibited or strongly discouraged?

When Selecting a Dive Operator

- Do tours respect all local guidelines, laws, regulations, and customs?
- Are local dive guides and divemasters hired where possible and appropriate?
- Are pre-dive talks offered by knowledgeable divemasters? Do they educate divers about the special features of the dive sites and reinforce rules for divers, such as: maintaining neutral buoyancy; maintaining control of lines, gauges, and accessories [so as not to damage the reef]; no touching, standing on, or collecting coral; no feeding or handling fish or other living organisms; abiding by any fishing or game regulations?
- Are mooring buoys used when possible and anchors never dropped onto coral reefs?
- Are engines well-maintained to avoid release of petroleum onto coral reefs?
- Is all sewage disposed of in a way that does not affect the nutrient balance of the reef ecosystems?
- Are environmentally sound methods of trash disposal used on boats and on land?
- Are special provisions made for disposal of harmful substances, such as chemicals used for film processing?
- Do tour operators limit the group size and frequency of dives?
- Do divemasters rotate dive sites to avoid over-using a particular site?
- Do divemasters verify the proficiency of new divers before allowing them to dive at fragile or difficult dive sites?

—Coral Reef Alliance (see chapter 10, Resources, for contact information)

Above and right: Even young children can feel like scuba divers using a flotation vest that keeps them on the surface but breathing compressed air through a regulator, just like mom.

FAMILY ACTIVITIES

Because youngsters must be at least 15 for full certification and 12 for limited junior certification, scuba diving is not a family activity in the way that skiing, fishing, or a trip to a theme park is. Water play when youngsters are quite small and snorkeling when they get older are great ways to introduce children to the water world. Jennifer King of the WSA—herself a mom—offers a checklist for enjoying the water with your children when they are small and preparing them to dive when they are older—see right.

In addition to these traditional tips by women who dive and want to share their passion with their families, other steps are being taken to get kids diving. Several manufacturers make a foam-filled BC-style vest that comes in various sizes and accommodates a small scuba tank, enabling children to breathe through a regulator while paddling on the surface. Aqua Lung calls its model SASY (Supplied Air Snorkeling for Youth); because it has no inflation/deflation device, SASY prevents children from submerging, but they do look and feel like divers. (SNUBA and Hookah are two brands of surface-supplied air, in which divers are tethered to a topside tank.)

Another development is PADI's "Bubble Maker" course, which is designed to give children between ages 8 and 12 years a sample of scuba diving in a pool or on a beach. The most important element is that children dive no deeper than 8 feet—and always with supervision. Being a Bubble Maker in a pool provides the feeling of diving, and going on a very shallow beach dive is

INTRODUCING YOUR CHILDREN TO SCUBA

I. Snorkeling as a family activity to help children appreciate the marine world

A. Children enjoy even the smallest fish and most barren dive spot!

B. You can snorkel in warm or cold water, at a resort, or right at home

C. Very small children (age two or three) can be introduced to the water on a boogie board with an underwater viewer

II. Starting Out

A. The right gear is essential—hypothermia, small faces, and discomfort will cause a child to quit

B. Learn how to size equipment for children

C. Take equipment one step at a time; forget about the snorkel and fins at first

D. Flotation devices: ScubaPro's snorkeling vest, wetsuit, and boogie board

III. Pool Training

A. Nonswimming children can use the Little Xtra suit for flotation or lie on a boogie board

B. Work with the mask: fitting, defogging, SlapStrap, clearing

C. Teach kids how to use the snorkel: clearing, attaching to mask

D. Use fins in the pool; different kicks for older kids

E. Skin-diving techniques for older children: the pike and tuck dives

F. Ear-clearing techniques

G. Use pennies, weighted hoops, and other toys for training

IV. Pre-Open-Water Dive

A. Use videos or books to show marine life and identify fish

B. Underwater chart with fish on it, underwater slate for writing, mesh bag for collecting

C. Rehearse proper dive and boat etiquette

D. Life jackets for smaller children

IV. Open-Water Dive

A. Calm-water conditions recommended for first trips

B. Use boat ladder and ramp

C. Possible disorientation in deeper water

D. Point out dangerous plants and animals to avoid

E. Getting in the water, using the buoy line, currents

F. Maintain control of the child while in the water

G. Solve problems such as flooded masks, surface chop, fear

H. Enjoy the marine life and beauty of the reef

I. Use a camera or video to document the child's snorkel trip

—Jennifer King, Women's Scuba Association

Snorkeling can be a beautiful end unto itself or an introduction, or adjunct, to scuba diving.

enough to see some fish, underwater rock formations, and even coral in some places.

In addition to Club Med, which is well-known as a family-friendly group of resorts with excellent children's programs, enabling parents to dive or participate in other adult sports, there are selected resorts and destinations that are appropriate for families. Rascals in Paradise is a tour operator specializing in finding just such destinations around the world. If your teenager is into diving but not into traveling with you, Broadreach, a specialist in summer diving and underwater ecology trips, is an option. For contact information, see chapter 10, Resources.

Snorkeling

For me and many other divers, snorkeling is the first step to the beauty of the underwater world. With clear water and a mask, snorkel, and fins, you can see 20 feet or so beneath the surface. Not only is snorkeling a fine diversion in its own right, but it's also a skill-builder. If you aren't completely comfortable in the water, snorkeling helps you become more at ease. You can snorkel without the surface intervals that diving requires, and you can snorkel just before you pack up and get on a plane. By snorkeling on the surface, combined with occasionally taking a lungful of air and swimming down to take a closer look at the wonders underwater, you truly will enhance your diving ability.

THE BOTTOM LINE ON BOTTOM TIME

You can read about diving, you can pore over exquisite underwater photographs in exquisitely printed coffee-table books, you can tune into every undersea nature show that the Discovery Channel, National Geographic, or the Public Broadcasting System beams your way. But nothing—I repeat, *nothing*—can match the magnificence, magic, and mystery of being there and gliding through an exotic and ethereal environment. Yes, I know there's a lot to learn about gear, physiology, and diving technique, and I know that sometimes diving doesn't seem worth the bother. And sometimes, too, a situation will be scary enough so that even as an experienced diver, you'll bail out of the dive. But every one of those concerns is washed away by the wonderful world beneath the waves. I've overcome the worries, as have millions of other women. We're all hooked on diving, and once you give it a try, chances are you will be, too.

Chapter 9

Adjustable Fins. Fins with forefoot pockets and adjustable heel straps

Alternate Air Source. Emergency air source, separate from the tank and regulator system. See *pony bottle*

Aluminum-80. *Dive tank*, which is a cylinder holding 80 cubic feet of *compressed air*

Ambient Pressure. Air pressure that has been reduced by the *regulator* to be usable and breathable

Analog Instruments. Instruments with gauges that are needles on dials (as opposed to digital readouts)

Artificial Reef. A cleaned-up ship, airplane, concrete culvert, or other large object that has been submerged offshore to provide habitat for marine plants and animals

Ascent Line/Descent Line. A line suspended from a *dive boat* or buoy to allow divers to control their ascent or descent rate

Auxiliary Second Stage. Backup *second stage* of a *regulator* that allows two divers to share air from one tank in order to ascend safely; also called an *octopus*

Back-Roll Entry. A *seated entry*, done by rolling backward into the water from the side of a small boat

Barotrauma. A medical term describing the effect of unequal pressure as the diver descends, such as abdominal barotrauma, dental barotrauma, and ear barotrauma

BC or BCD. See *buoyancy compensator*

The Bends. The colloquial term for *decompression sickness* or *decompression illness*

Boat Dive. Open-water dive from a boat

Body Suit. See *dive skins*

Booties. See *dive booties*

Bottle. Colloquial term for scuba *tank* or *cylinder*

Bottom Time. The length of time in minutes from the beginning of the descent to the beginning of the ascent

Buddy. Diving partner

Buddy Breathing. Two divers sharing an air source by passing a single *regulator* between them

Buoyancy. Flotation caused by upward force that prevents an object from sinking in water

Buoyancy Check. A surface skill in which divers, fully equipped and weighted, check whether descent is possible

Buoyancy Compensator. Multipurpose inflatable vest that holds the *tank*, allowing the wearer to float on the surface and to be neutrally buoyant underwater (referred to as a BC or BCD)

Buoyancy Control Device. See *buoyancy compensator*

C-Card. Colloquial term for *certification card*

Certification. Qualification to dive by passing a skills and theory test, according to the curriculum of a *certifying agency*

Certification Card. The official document from a *certifying agency* indicating that a diver has mastered a certain level of proficiency

Certifying Agency. A dive organization that sets a curriculum, trains divers, and establishes testing procedures for new and advanced divers of various levels

Clearing the Mask. Expelling water that has accumulated in the mask

Compressed Air. The nitrogen-oxygen mixture, under pressure, used to fill dive *tanks*

Confined Water. Swimming pool or custom pool in a dive shop, as opposed to *open water*

Console. See *instrument console*

Cyalume. Chemical that glows in the dark and that can be used under water; sold in glow sticks for night diving

Cylinder. Tank for *compressed air*

DCI, DCS. See *decompression illness, decompression sickness*

Decompression. Controlled ascent timed to allow the body to adjust from the pressure of being underwater

Decompression Illness. An umbrella term for *decompression sickness* and lung overexpansion

Decompression Sickness. A painful and potentially serious condition caused when nitrogen bubbles remain in the tissues and bloodstream

Deep Dive. For recreational divers, dive approaching the maximum depth of 130 feet; also, the first deeper and shorter dive of two consecutive dives

Deep Diving. Highly technical dives deeper than 190 feet, requiring *decompression*

Depth Gauge. The instrument that measures and displays how deep below the water surface a diver is

Digital Instruments. Instruments that provide information on a numerical display (as opposed to *analog instruments*)

Dive Boat. Boat equipped for diving, usually featuring at least a *dive platform* on the stern and some method of holding the *cylinders* while underway

Dive Booties. Protective rubber-soled footwear made of neoprene, designed to be worn with *adjustable fins*

Dive Computer. Electronic instrument that monitors dive depth and air pressure, displays current information digitally, and stores *dive profile* data

Dive Flag. Red banner with a white stripe from the upper left to lower right corner; affixed to a dive boat or buoy to warn other boaters that divers are below; also a symbol for scuba diving

Dive Hood. A garment worn over the head to provide insulation and protection

Dive Light. Specialty flashlight in a waterproof housing for night diving or diving in dark places such as wrecks and caves

Divemaster. An advanced level of dive certification; often a dive leader or assistant to a dive instructor

Dive Plan. The planned maximum depth and *bottom time* of a dive

Dive Platform. A platform on the stern of a *dive boat* that allows divers to enter and exit the water

Dive Profile. The statistics of a dive, including maximum depth, *bottom time*, and air consumed

Dive Skin. One-piece Lycra suit (sometimes lined with Polartec fleece), most suitable for warm-water diving

Dive Tables. Charts in which each dive's *bottom time* and maximum depth are converted into *pressure groups* that determine subsequent dives

Drift Diving. A type of *boat dive* in which the divers descend at one location and move in the direction of the current, followed by the *dive boat*, which picks them up at another location at the end of the dive

Dry Suit. Waterproofed *exposure suit* that is filled with air to provide for cold-water diving

Dump Valve. A valve activated by a pull cord that quickly releases all air from the *BC*

Enriched Air. A mixture of air with more oxygen than occurs naturally; also called *nitrox* or oxygen-enriched air

Equalizing. Forcing air into ear passages and *mask* to relieve pressure during the descent and to compensate for the increase in *hydrostatic pressure*

Exhaust Valve. The one-way valve in the *regulator* that allows air to escape when the diver exhales

Exposure Protection. Function of *wetsuits*, *dry suits*, and—to a lesser extent—*dive skins*

Exposure Suit. A divewear category consisting of wetsuits, dry suits, and even dive skins

Farmer Jane. Women's version of the *Farmer John*

Farmer John. *Wetsuit* bottoms resembling overalls that extend over the upper body

Fins. "Flippers" that attach to the diver's feet for efficient movement through the water

First Stage. The part of the regulator that is attached to the *tank* that begins reducing the pressure of the air transmitted to the diver through the air hose

Free Diving. Formalized *skin diving*, usually to greater depths

Full-Foot Fins. *Fins* that encase the entire bare foot

Full Suit. One-piece *wetsuit* with long sleeves and long legs

Giant Stride. A long step off a boat's *dive platform* or dock for entry into the water

Glow Stick. See *Cyalume*

Hydrostatic Pressure. Water pressure

Hyperbaric Chamber. A medical facility that can be pressurized and gradually depressurized to treat a diver with *decompression sickness*

Hyperthermia. Overheating, when the body's core temperature rises above 98.6°F; also called heat exhaustion

Hypothermia. A body chill, when the body's core temperature falls below 98.6°F

Inflator Hose. Hose that is part of the *BC* and attaches to the tank to inflate the bladder; also features a deflator button to release air from it

Inlet Valve. The one-way valve in the *regulator* that allows air to flow from the *tank* when the diver inhales

Instrument Console. Submersible instrument panel that monitors depth and air supply and often compass direction

Integrated Weight Design. *BC* with pockets to hold weights as an alternative to a separate weight belt

Lead. Colloquial term for dive weights

Lift Bag. A bag resembling a hot-air balloon and tied to an object to be raised from the sea bottom and inflated from a regulator

Liveaboard. A cabin cruiser than combines the features of a day-excursion *dive boat* with cabins providing overnight accommodations

Logbook. A dive diary, in which a diver logs dive site, *dive profile*, and other noteworthy features

Lube Suit. Lightweight undersuit that enables divers to slip a wetsuit on and off easily

Mask. Goggle-like device that fits over the eyes and nose creating an airspace and enabling the diver to focus underwater and *equalize* during the descent

Mask Squeeze. Uncomfortable swelling of the tissue around the eyes when a diver has failed to *equalize* her *mask*

Mixed Gases. Formulations of air not found in nature, such as *nitrox*; mixtures to extend advanced divers' range, depth, and *bottom time*

Mouthpiece. The portion of a second-stage regulator or snorkel that fits into the mouth

Multilevel Dive. A single dive in which the diver spends time at various depths

Nitrogen Narcosis. A feeling of disorientation similar to drunkenness that can develop with increased nitrogen pressure in the body; also called *rapture of the deep*

Nitrox. Oxygen-enriched air, diving with which requires specialty training

No-Decompression Diving. For technical divers, dives to 190 feet and for recreational divers, dives to a maximum of 130 feet, which do not require *decompression* stops during the ascent, as *deep dives* do

Octopus. The spare or back-up *second stage* of the *regulator*

Open Water. Ocean, lake, or other natural body of water; opposite of *confined water*

O-Ring. A pliable ring used as a high-pressure seal for tank valves

Overhead Environments. Underwater caverns, caves, shipwrecks, or any other situation with a ceiling that makes it impossible for divers to ascend directly to the surface

Oxygen Toxicity. Reaction of the body to excess oxygen levels

Pelagics. Deep-water fish and mammal species that live in open seas rather than shallow, offshore waters

Pony Tank or Pony Bottle. A small, redundant air-source system designed so that the diver can ascend safely to the surface in the highly unlikely event that the *regulator* fails

Pressure Gauge. Instrument that measures a diver's depth underwater

Pressure Group. A mathematical combination of a dive's duration and depth, which determines the depth and duration of subsequent dives

Primary Second Stage. The main *second stage* of the *regulator*, which the diver uses to breathe (as opposed to the *octopus* or auxiliary second stage)

Purge Valve. A one-way valve that enables a diver to expel water from the *regulator* or *mask*

Rapture of the Deep. Colloquial expression for *nitrogen narcosis*

Rebreather. An underwater unit that recycles breathing gas by removing carbon dioxide and adding oxygen

Recreational Dive Tables. Standardized tables including *pressure groups* and required *surface intervals* that allow recreational divers to dive safely and avoid *decompression illness* under all conditions

Redundant Air Source. *Pony bottle*

Regulator. The device that converts high-pressure air in the *tank* to usable pressure for breathing and to inflate the *BCD*; see *ambient pressure*

Reverse Block. A condition that occurs when expanding air cannot escape from an air space, including the ears and sinuses, during the ascent; also called *reverse squeeze* and ear *barotrauma*

Safety Stop. Remaining 15 feet below the surface for three minutes on the ascent, to begin eliminating excess nitrogen from the body

Seated Entry. Entering the water from the side of a pool or a low *dive platform*, starting from a seated position

Second Stage. The part of the *regulator* that is attached to the *mouthpiece* to reduce pressure to a point where it is breathable

Self-Rescue Skills. Includes skills such as *regulator* recovery, *mask-clearing*, *weight-belt* and *BC* handling, and others that are practiced if something goes amiss underwater

Semi-Dry Suit. A wetsuit designed to limit the amount of sea water that can enter the suit.

Setting Up. The process of assembling equipment (i.e., *BC*, *regulator*, and *tank*) in preparation for a dive

Shore Dive. A walk-in dive from a beach

Shortie. Short-legged, one-piece *wetsuit* (either short- or long-sleeved)

Skills. A catch-all name for specific activities used in diving, including mask-clearing and removing and putting on various items of equipment underwater

Skin Diving. A shallow dive done without scuba gear and on a single breath

Sniff Test. Technique for testing *mask* fit by placing it against the face and inhaling through the nose

Snorkel. Plastic tube that allows a snorkeler swimming facedown on the surface to breathe; also used by scuba divers on the surface before and after a dive; also known as a *tube*

Spare Air. See *pony tank* or *pony bottle*

Split Fin. Fin with split rather than solid blade, designed to enhance propulstion through the water and worn with booties

Surface Interval. The length of time at the surface between dives

Tank. An aluminum or steel *cylinder* for *compressed air*

Technical Diving. Highly advanced levels of diving in situations that call for special training and sometimes special equipment

Tube. Colloquial term for *snorkel*

Wall. An underwater cliff face at the edge of the continental shelf

Weight Belt. Webbed nylon belt onto which dive *weights* are threaded

Weights. Lead weights (solid or pellets) used to counteract the natural *buoyancy* of the diver, *exposure suit*, and other equipment

Wetsuit. A one-piece, zip-up, neoprene *exposure suit* (sometimes lined in Polartec fleece), available in different thicknesses (measured in millimeters) to help a diver retain body heat

Wreck Diving. A dive to explore an underwater shipwreck or airplane wreck

Chapter 10

RESOURCES

ORGANIZATIONS

Training and Certifying Agencies

Accessible Waves (1994, as
Desiderata Snorkel
and Scuba)
1990 Poplar Ave.
Boulder CO 80304
303-447-3005
Special-needs divers.

ACUC International (ACUC)
(1968)
1264 Osprey Dr.
Ancaster ON
L9G 3L2 Canada
905-648-5500
Fax 905-648-5440
E-mail: acuc@acuc.ca

www.acuc.ca
Entry-level through advanced.

American Nitrox Divers
International (ANDI) (1989)
74 Woodcleft Ave.
Freeport NY 11520
516-546-2026
Fax 516-546-6010
E-mail: andihq@aol.com
www.andihq.com
Advanced.

Handicapped Scuba Association
(HSA International)
(1981)
1104 El Prado
San Clemente CA 92672
949-498-6128
Fax 949-498-6128
E-mail: hsa@hsascuba.com

www.hsascuba.dom
Special-needs divers.

International Association of
Free Divers (IAFD)
(1999)
10344 Overseas Hwy.
Key Largo FL 33037
305-453-9588
Fax 305-453-0635
E-mail: DixDives@aol.com
www.freediving.net/iafd/htm

International Association of
Nitrox and Technical Divers
(IANTD) (1985)
9628 NE 2nd Ave., Suite D
Miami Shores FL 33138
305-751-4873
Fax 305-751-3958
E-mail: iantdhq@ix.netcom.com

www.iantd.com
Advanced.

International Diving Educators
    Association (IDEA) (1952, as
    Florida Skin Divers
    Association)
P.O. Box 8427
Jacksonville FL 32239
904-744-5554
Fax 904-743-5425
E-mail: ideahq@aol.com
www.idea-scubadiving.com

National Association for Cave
    Diving (NACD) (1968)
P.O. Box 14492
Gainesville FL 32640
352-495-6223
Fax 352-495-6223
E-mail: ecasson@hp.ufl.edu
www.safecavediving.com
Advanced.

National Association of Scuba
    Diving Schools (NASDS)
    (1961)
(Merged with Scuba Schools
    International in 1999; see that
    listing for contact information)

National Association of
    Underwater Instructors (NAUI)
    (1960)
9942 Currie Davis Dr., Suite H
Tampa FL 33619
813-628-6284
800-553-6284
Fax 813-628-8253
E-mail: nauihq@nauiww.org
www.naui.org and
    www.nauiww.org
Entry-level through advanced.

Professional Association of Diving
    Instructors (PADI) (1966)

30151 Tomas St.
Rancho Santa Margarita CA
    92688
949-858-7234
800-729-7234
www.padi.com
Entry-level through advanced.

Professional Diving Instructors
    Corporation (PDIC) (1975)
1554 Gardner Ave.
Scranton PA 18509
717-342-1480
Fax 717-342-1276
E-mail: info@pdic-intl.com
www.pdic-intl.com
Advanced.

Professional Scuba Association
    (PSA) (1987)
9487 NW 115th Ave.
Ocala FL 34482-1007
352-368-7974
Fax 352-351-1924
E-mail: staff@mrscuba.com
www.mrscuba.com
Advanced.

Scuba Diving International (SDI)
    and Technical Diving
    International (TDI) (1994)
18 Elm St.
Topsham ME 04086
207-729-4201
Fax 207-729-4453
E-mail: worldhq@tdisci.com
www.tdisdu.com
SDI is entry-level through
    advanced; TDI is advanced.

Scuba Schools International (SSI)
    (1970)
2619 Canton Ct.
Fort Collins CO 80525-4498
970-482-0883
800-892-2702

Fax 970-482-6157
E-mail: admin@ssiusa.com
www.ssiusa.com
Entry-level through advanced.

World Association of Scuba
    Instructors (WASI) (1997)
134 S. Main St., Suite M140
Salt Lake City UT 84101
801-363-9274
Fax 801-359-4461
E-mail: wasi@divewasi.com
www.divewasi.com
Entry-level through advanced.

YMCA Scuba (1959)
5825 Live Oak Pkwy., Suite 2A
Norcross GA 30093
770-662-5172
888-464-9622
Fax 770-242-9059
E-mail: scubaymca@aol.com
www.ymcascuba.org
Entry-level through advanced.

Divers' Organizations

Institute of Diving and Museum of
    Man in the Sea
17314 Panama City Beach Pkwy.
Panama City Beach FL 32413-
    2020
850-235-4101
Fax 850-235-4101

National Association of Black
    Scuba Divers
1605 Crittenden St. NE
Washington DC 20017
800-521-NABS (800-521-6227)
Fax 202-526-2907
E-mail: contactus@nabsdivers.org
www.nabsdivers.org

PADI Diving Society
(See Professional Association of

Diving Instructors for contact information)

Recreational Divers Association (RDA)
3510 Lester Ct.
Lilburn GA 30047
770-982-4194
Fax 770-985-0175
E-mail: service@recreational-divers.com
www.recreational-divers.com

Underwater Society of America
P.O. Box 628
Daly City CA 94017
650-583-8492
Fax 650-583-0614
E-mail: croseusoa@aol.com
www.underwater-society.org

Women's Scuba Association (WSA)
6966 S. Atlantic Ave.
New Smyrna Beach FL 32169
904-426-5757
Fax 904-426-5744
E-mail: kingfish@ucnsb.net
www.jscuba.com/wsa

Divers' Insurance

Divers Alert Network (DAN)
6 W. Colony Pl.
Durham NC 27705
800-446-2671
Fax 919-490-6630
www.diversalertnetwork.org

Divers Equipment Protection Program (DEPP)
c/o International Association of Nitrox and Technical Divers (IANTD)
9628 NE 2nd Ave., Suite D
Miami Shores FL 33138-2767
888-678-4096

E-mail: iantdhq@ix-netcom.com
www.iantd.com

Commercial Diving Career Training

Barry University
11300 NE 2nd Ave.
Miami Shores FL 33161-6695
305-899-3100
800-695-2279
Fax 305-899-2971
E-mail: admissions@pcsa01.edu
www.barry.edu

Divers Academy of the Eastern Seaboard
2500 Broadway
Camden NJ 08104
609-966-1871

Diver's Institute of Technology
P.O. Box 70667
Seattle WA 98107
800-634-8377
E-mail: dit@wolfnet.com
www.Diveweb.com/DIT

Eastern Academy of Scuba Education (instructor school)
416 Miracle Mile
Vero Beach FL 32960
561-562-2883
800-732-9685
E-mail: cliff@deepsix.com
www.deepsix.com

The Ocean Corporation
10840 Rockley Rd.
Houston TX 77099
800-321-0298
www.ocorp.com

Pro Dive International
515 Seabreeze Blvd.
Bahia Mar Yachting Resort
Fort Lauderdale FL 33316

954-761-8915
888-776-3483
Fax 954-761-8915
E-mail: prodive@icanect.net
www.pro-dive.com

South East Diving Institute
14601 Orange Ave.
Fort Pierce FL 34945
561-466-3388
Fax 561-466-3444

Marine Conservation Organizations

American Oceans Campaign (headquarters)
600 Pennsylvania Ave. SE, Suite 210
Washington DC 20003
202-544-3526
Fax 202-544-5625
E-mail: aocdc@wizard.net
www.americanoceans.org

American Oceans Campaign (L.A. Office)
6030 Wilshire Blvd., Suite 400
Los Angeles CA 90036
323-936-8242
Fax 323-936-2320
E-mail: aoc@earthlink.com
www.americanoceans.org

Caribbean Conservation Corp.
4424 NW 13th St., Suite A-1
Gainesville FL 32679
352-373-6441
800-678-7853
Fax 352-375-2449
E-mail: ccc@cccturtle.org
www.cccturtle.org

Center for Marine Conservation
1725 DeSales St. NW, Suite 600
Washington DC 20036
202-429-5609

Fax 202-872-0619
E-mail: cmc@dccmc.org
www.cmc-ocean.org

Center for Oceanic Research and
    Education (CORE)
245 Western Ave.
Essex MA 01929
978-768-4560
www.coreresearch.org

Cetacean Society International
P.O. Box 953
Georgetown CT 06829
203-431-1606
Fax 203-431-1606
www.elfnetla.elfi.com/csihome.html

Coastal Ecosystems Research
    Foundation
2648 Tennis Crescent
Vancouver BC
V6T 2E1 Canada
604-224-4729
877-223-2373
E-mail: info@cerf.bc.ca
www.cerf.bc.ca

Coral Reef Alliance (CORAL)
2014 Shattuck Ave.
Berkeley CA 94704
510-848-0110
Fax 510-848-3720
E-mail: info@coral.org
www.coral.org

Cousteau Society
870 Greenbriar Cir., Suite 402
Chesapeake VA 23320
800-441-4395
www.cousteau.org

Earthwatch Institute
680 Mt. Auburn St.
P.O. Box 9104
Watertown MA 02471-9104
800-776-0188

Fax 617-926-8532
E-mail: info@earthwatch.org
www.earthwatch.org

Greenpeace USA
1436 U St. NW
Washington DC 20009
202-462-1177
Fax 202-462-4507
E-mail: greenpeace.usa@wdc.
    greenpeace.org
www.greenpeace.org

National Ocean Service
1305 East-West Hwy.
Silver Spring MD 20910
301-713-3074
www.nos.noaa.gov

National Oceanic and
    Atmospheric Administration
    (NOAA)
14th St. and Constitution Ave.
    NW, Room 6013
Washington DC 20230
202-482-6090
Fax 202-482-3154
www.nos.noaa.gov

Oceanwatch
2101 Wilson Blvd., Suite 900
Arlington VA 22201
703-351-7444
Fax 703-351-7472
E-mail: oceanwatch@aol.com
www.enviroweb.org/oceanwatch

Project AWARE Foundation
c/o PADI
30151 Tomas St.
Rancho Santa Margarita CA
    92688
949-858-7234
800-729-7234
Fax 949-858-7521
E-mail: aware@padi.com
www.padi.com

Reef Ball Foundation
603 River Overlook Rd.
Woodstock GA 30188
770-752-0202
Fax 770-360-1328
E-mail: kkirbo@hotmail.com
www.reefball.org

Reef Environmental Education
    Foundation (R.E.E.F.)
P.O. Box 246
Key Largo FL 33037
305-451-0312
Fax 305-451-0028
E-mail: reefhq@aol.com
www.reef.org

Reef Relief
201 William St.
P.O. Box 430
Key West FL 33041
305-294-3100
Fax 305-293-9515
E-mail: reef@bellsouth.net
www.reefrelief.org

Sea Turtle Survival League
(See Caribbean Conservation
    Organization for contact infor-
    mation)

Shark Research Institute
P.O. Box 40
Princeton NJ 08540
609-921-3522
Fax 609-921-1505
www.sharks.org

Western Pacific Fisheries
    Coalition
970 N. Kalaheo Ave.,
    Suite C-413
Kailua HI 96734
808-254-5900
Fax 808-254-5404
E-mail: bob@westpacfisheries.net

Marine sanctuaries

For information about these underwater parks, dive regulations, permitted dive operators, and volunteer diving opportunities, call each sanctuary or log onto the NOAA website (see entry page 132). Three parks discourage diving, but all are noteworthy for trying to sustain healthy seas. America's sea havens and their highlights are as follows:

- Channel Islands National Marine Sanctuary, Southern California. Five islands in the California Bight, 100 shipwrecks, walls, pinnacles, caves, abundant cold-water sea life, including sea lions. 805-966-7107.

- Cordell Bank, a 200-mile chain of islands, off San Francisco. Pacific salmon, rockfish, seals, 33 marine mammal species (diving discouraged). 415-561-6616.

- Fagatele Bay National Marine Sanctuary, American Samoa. Coral reef (200 species of Indo-Pacific coral), large population and variety of tropical reef fish, humpback whales. 011-68-4-633-7354.

- Florida Keys National Marine Sanctuary, including 18 Sanctuary Preservation Areas in a 200-mile chain of islands between South Florida and Key West. Diving (off-limits to fishing and specimen-collecting), mangrove and sea grass habitats. 305-743-2357.

- Flower Banks National Marine Sanctuary, Freeport, Texas. Northernmost coral reef system in the United States; 22 species of coral, 300 species of fish, 400 species of invertebrates. 409-779-2705.

- Gulf of the Farallones, a 200-mile chain of islands, Monterey Bay, California. Coastal habitats and offshore islands, anchovies, crab, rockfish, flatfish, 33 species of marine mammals, one fifth of California's harbor seals (diving discouraged). 415-561-6616.

- Gray's Reef National Marine Sanctuary, off Sapelo Island, Georgia. Encrusted limestone ledges, caves, one of the country's largest reefs near shore, 150 species of fish. 912-598-2345.

- Hawaiian Islands Humpback Whale National Marine Sanctuary, to the 100-fathom contour around the main islands. Humpback whales (boats and aircraft are prohibited from interfering), lava tubes, caverns, distinctive Pacific reef and pelagic species (some found only here). 800-831-4888, 808-879-2818.

- Monitor National Marine Sanctuary, off Cape Hatteras, North Carolina. Remains of the Civil War ironclad, the *USS Monitor*. 757-599-3122.

- Monterey Bay National Marine Sanctuary, central California coast. Twenty-seven species of rare or endangered marine life, kelp beds, salmon, rockfish, sea lions, sea otters, squid, anchovies. 408-647-4201.

- Olympic Coast National Marine Sanctuary, Cape Flattery, Washington. Kelp forests, fish, shellfish, 29 species of marine mammals (including killer and gray whales), 150 shipwrecks. 360-457-6622.

- Stellwagen Bank National Marine Sanctuary, Cape Cod, Massachusetts. Northern right whales (only about 300 exist), humpback whales, popular for commercial whale-watching (diving discouraged). 508-747-1691.

Trade associations

Diving Equipment and Marketing Association (DEMA)
2050 Santa Cruz St., Suite 160
Anaheim CA 92805-6399
714-939-6399
Fax 714-939-6398
www.dema.org

Recreational Scuba Training Council (RSTC)
3047 Joan St.
Land o' Lakes FL 34649
813-996-6582

Women's Scuba Association (WSA) and Women's Equipment Test Team (WETT)
6966 S. Atlantic Ave.
New Smyrna Beach FL 32169
904-426-5757
Fax 904-426-5744
E-mail: kingfish@ucnsb.net
www.jscuba.com/wsa

MEDIA

Books

Guidebooks to dive sites in particular areas abound, as do books on serious technical diving. Purveyors of those books are listed in the publishers listing. The following is a sampling of books that are of general interest or geared to new divers or to those interested in the undersea world.

Bane, Michael. *Diving on the Edge.* New York: Lyons Press, 1998.

Cardone, Bonnie. *The Fireside Diver: An Anthology of Underwater Adventure.* Locust Valley NY: Aqua Quest, 1996.

Earle, Sylvia. *Sea Change: A Message of the Oceans.* New York: Putnam, 1994.

Earle, Sylvia. *The Oceans.* New York: McGraw-Hill, 1999.

Earle, Sylvia, and Henry Wolcott. *Wild Ocean.* Washington DC: National Geographic Books, 1999.

Graver, Dennis K. *Scuba Diving.* Champaign IL: Human Kinetics, 1999.

Kitrell, Ed, Casey, and Jim. *Down Time: Great Writing on Diving.* Austin TX: Look Away Books, 1998.

Mountain, Alan. *The Diver's Handbook.* New York: Lyons Press, 1997.

Newman, John. *Scuba Diving and Snorkeling for Dummies.* Foster City CA: IDG Books, 1999.

Richardson, Drew (editor-in-chief). *The Encyclopedia of Recreational Diving.* Santa Ana CA: PADI, second edition, 1998. Also available on CD-ROM.

Saunders, Dave. *Scuba Diving: Know the Sport.* Mechanicsburg PA: Stackpole Books, 1996.

Valentine, Reg, and Sharron Davies. *Learn Scuba Diving in a Weekend.* New York: Knopf, 1998.

CD-ROMs

The Encyclopedia of Recreational Diving—Multimedia (CD-ROM version of *The Encyclopedia of Recreational Diving*). PADI; see contact information above

Explore the Blue Planet (information on worldwide dive destinations and tour operators specializing in diving).
Sports-N-Fun
P.O. Box 1773
Boulder CO 80308-0663
303-444-8582
Fax 303-998-0272
E-mail: outoftheblue1@
   juno.com
www.sports-n-fun.com

Dive book publishers and catalogs

AquaQuest Publications
P.O. Box 700
Locust Valley NY 11560
518-759-0476
800-933-8989
Fax 516-759-4519
E-mail: aquaquest@aol.com
Publishes and distributes dive guidebooks, fish-identification books, technical books, and videos

Aqua Explorers
980 Church St.
Baldwin NY 11510
800-695-7585
516-868-2658
Fax 516-868-2658
E-mail: Wreckvalle@aol.com
www.aquaexplorers.com

Bennett Video Corporation
730 Washington St.
Marina del Rey CA 90292
310-821-3329

800-733-8862
Fax 310-821-8074
Distributes instructional, travel, adventure, and even humor videos

Best Publishing Company
P.O. Box 30100
2355 N. Steeves Blvd.
Flagstaff AZ 86003-0100
520-527-1055
800-468-1055
Fax 520-526-0370
E-mail: divedooks@bestpub.com
Distributes books on diving history, adventure, travel, careers, equipment, medicine, safety, photography, and more

Fielding Worldwide
4455 Torrance Blvd., Suite 827
Torrance CA 90503
310-372-4474
Fax 310-376-8064
E-mail:
   fielding@fieldingtravel.com
www.fieldingtravel.com
Publishes Periplus Edition series of dive guidebooks

Lonely Planet
150 Linden St.
Oakland CA 94607
800-275-8555
www.lonelyplanet.com
Publishes Pisces Books series of dive guidebooks

Passport Books
4255 W. Touhy Ave.
Lincolnwood IL 60646-1975
847-679-5500
800-323-4900
Fax 847-679-2494/800-998-3103
E-mail: ntcpub@tribune.com
Publishes a series of guidebooks in the Dive Site series

Note that each certifying agency (see pages 129–30) publishes manuals, perhaps CD-ROMs or videotapes, and other training materials, available through affiliated dive shops.

Magazines and Newsletters

Alert Diver
c/o DAN
See Divers Alert Network (page 131) for contact information

Discover Diving
P.O. Box 83727
San Diego CA 92138
619-697-0703
Fax 619-697-0123

Dive Training
P.O. Box 14236
Parkville MO 64152-9901
816-741-5151
www.divetrainingmag.com

Immersed (technical diving magazine)
Subscriptions
P.O. Box 638
Chester NY 10918-9914
www.immersed.com

New Diver
Available free at dive centers, see *Rodale's Scuba Diving* for contact information or visit <www. NewDiver.com> for up-to-date information on certifying agencies, equipment, and what to expect during your dive training

Rodale's Scuba Diving
Subscriptions:
P.O. Box 7576

Red Oak IA 51591-2576
800-666-0016
Editorial:
6600 Abercorn St., Suite 208
Savannah GA 31405
912-351-0855
Fax 912-3561-0735
E-mail: scubadiving@aol.com
www.scubadiving.com

Skin Diver
6420 Wilshire Blvd.
Los Angeles CA 90048
323-782-2960
Fax 323-728-2121

Sport Diver
Subscriptions:
P.O. Box 420745
Palm Coast FL 32142-8583
Editorial:
330 W. Canton Ave.
Winter Park FL 32789
407-628-4802
Fax 407-628-7061
E-mail: sportdvr@gate.net

Undercurrent
Subscriptions:
P.O. Box 1658
Sausalito CA 94966
415-461-5906
800-326-1896
Editorial:
P.O. Box 90215
Austin TX 78709
Fax 512-891-9813
E-mail: editor@
    undercurrent.org
www.undercurrent.org

Women Underwater
P.O. Box 2338
Flemington NJ 08822
908-788-9974
Fax 908-788-9582

E-mail: underh2o@ptd.net
www.WomenUnderwater.com

SPECIALIZED EQUIPMENT

BCs and Wetsuits Sized for Women

Aeroskin California
    (wetsuits only)
45 Olive St.
San Francisco CA 94109
415-346-4756
800-368-9255
Fax 415-346-4990/
    800-333368-9252
E-mail: aeroskin@aol.com
www.aeroskin.com

Aqua-Lung/U.S. Divers
3323 W. Warner Ave.
P.O. Box 25018
Santa Ana CA 92799-5018
714-540-8010
Fax 714-432-9340
www.usdivers.com

Body Glove (wetsuits only)
2860 California St.
Torrance CA 90503
310-320-7873
800-6788-7873
Fax 310-320-7889

Cressi-Sub-USA
    (Women's Technical BC)
10 Reuten Dr.
Closter NJ 07624
201-784-1005
Fax 201-784-1142
www.cressi-sub.it

Dacor
161 Northfield Rd.
Northfield IL 60093
847-446-555

Fax 847-446-7547
www.divedacor.com

Diveskins (wetsuits only)
7717 SW Nimbus Ave.
Beaverton OR 97008
503-644-2485
800-827-DIVE
Fax 503-644-2786/888-827-3483
E-mail: diveskin@teleport.co

Genesis Scuba (BCs only)
6204 Goodrich Rd.
Clarence Center NY 14032
716-741-4789
www.genesisscuba.com

International Divers (BCs only)
14747 Artesia Blvd., Unit 5F
La Mirada CA 90638
714-994-3900
800-257-2822
Fax 714-994-5342
E-mail: IDI@worldnet.att.net

Mares (BCs only)
1 Selleck St.
Norwalk CT 06855
203-855-0631
800-874-3236
Fax 800-253-8509
www.htmsport.com

Oceanic
2002 Davis St.
San Leandro CA 94577-1211
510-562-0500
Fax 510-569-5404
www.oceanicusa.com

ScubaPro
116-A Fessler St.
El Cajon CA 92020
619-402-1023
www.jwa.com/scubapro/

SeaQuest (BCs only)
2340 Cousteau Ct.
Vista CA 92083
760-727-8488
Fax 760-727-8459
www.sea-quest.com

Sherwood Scuba (BCs)
2111 Liberty Dr.
Niagara Falls NY 14304-3744
716-283-2270 ext. 3151
Fax 716-283-2356

TransPac (BCs and technical
   equipment)
117 W. Washington St.
Lake City FL 32055
904-752-1087
Fax 904-755-0613
www.dive-rite.com

Tusa/Tabata USA (BCs only)
2380 Mira Mar Ave.
Long Beach CA 90815
562-498-3708
Fax 562-498-1390
E-mail: info@exposonline.com
www.exposonline.com/
   scuba.tusa.html

Undersea Designs (wetsuits only)
2801 Via Cascada
Carlsbad CA 92008
760-434-8508
www.underseadesigns.com

Xcel Wetsuits (wetsuits only)
66-590 Kamehameha Hwy.
Halweiwa HI 96712
808-637-6239
800-637-2935
Fax 808-637-9233

Custom Wetsuits

Harvey's Skindiving Suits
2505 S. 252nd St.

Kent WA 98032
206-824-1144
800-347-0054
Fax 206-824-3323
www.harveys-divesuits.com

Henderson Aquatics
301 Orange St.
Millville NJ 08332
856-825-4771
Fax 856-825-6378
E-mail: sales@hendersonusa.com
www.hendersonusa.com

O'Neill, Inc.
1071 41st St.
P.O. Box 6300
Santa Cruz CA 95063-6300
800-662-7873
800-538-0764 (outside California)
Fax 831-475-0544
www.teamoneill.com

Custom Mouthpieces

SeaCURE
5801 Washington Ave., Suite 100
Racine WI 53406-4098
608-328-8008
800-428-9494
Fax 414-884-7710
www.seacure1.com

Dry Suits

Aqua Lung/U.S. Divers
3323 W. Warner Ave.
P.O. Box 25018
Santa Ana CA 92799-5018
714-540-8010
Fax 714-432-9340
www.aqualung.com

Cochran Undersea Technology
1758 Firman Dr.
Richardson TX 75081
972-644-6284

Diving Unlimited International
(DUI)
1148 Delevan Dr.
San Diego CA 92102-2499
619-236-1203
800-325-8439
Fax 619-237-0278
www.DUI-online.com

Oceanic
See under BCs and Wetsuits
Sized for Women

Sea Lion/Respirex North America
2607 Spring Cypress Rd.
Spring TX 77288
281-350-1200
E-mail: slrespirex@aol.com

Prescription Mask Lenses

Curt Walker, Optician
3434 4th Ave.
San Diego CA 92103
619-299-2878
800-538-2878
Fax 619-299-9934
www.prescriptiondivemasks.com

Scuba Optics
1405 8th Ave.
Rock Falls IL 61071
815-625-7272
Fax 815-625-9735
E-mail: scubaopt@essex1.com

Rearview Mirror for Masks

Sport Divers Manufacturing
1923 NE 150th St.
Miami FL 33181
305-947-5692
Fax 305-947-9261
800-327-0244
E-mail: sportdivermfg@usa.net

Soft Weights

ScubaPro
116-A Fessler St.
El Cajon CA 92020
619-402-1023
www.jwa.com/scubapro

Sea Pearls
P.O. Box 204
Osseo MN 55369
612-424-5332
800-328-3852
Fax 612-424-2027/800-248-5430

Underwater Personal Heater

PATCO Service
2515 Glencoe Rd.
Baltimore MD 21234
410-444-4010
Fax 410-254-9566

Underwater Sign Language

Sea Signs
5288-B Eastgate Mall
San Diego CA 92121
619-677-0490
Fax 619-677-9762
E-mail: SuzSea@suzsea.com

Vented Earplugs

International Aquatic Traders
719 Swift St., Suite 100
Santa Cruz CA 95060
800-521-2082
Fax 888-507-7565

Wetsuit Accessory (Easy-on, Easy-off)

Lube Suit
11922 Westheimer, Suite 405
Houston TX 77077-6604
281-496-3444

Fax 281-870-1354
E-mail: LubeSuit@aol.com
www.lubesuit.com

Mail-Order Companies

Bennett Marine Video
730 Washington St.
Marina del Rey CA 90292
800-733-8862
Fax 310-827-8074
www.videoflicks.com/BMV/index.
html

Divers Casino (on-line, real-time
auction of dive products)
www.diverscasino.com

Dive Guide International
980 Vail View Dr., Suite B-211
Vail CO 81657
970-477-0342
800-786-5785
Fax 970-477-0343
E-mail: info@diveguide.com
www.divetravel.com

Divers Discount Supply
30161 Banderas #6
Rancho Santa Margarita CA 92688
800-34-SCUBA (800-347-2822)
Fax 949-459-9900
E-mail: info@diversdiscount.com
www.diversdiscount.com

LeisurePro
42 W. 18th St.
New York NY 10011
212-645-1234
800-637-6880
Fax 212-691-7286
E-mail: goleisure@aol.com
www.leisure-pro.com

Mr. Diver
P.O. Box 36

Big Sandy TN 38221
800-532-2228
E-mail: mrdiverinc@worldnet.
   att.net
www.mrdiver.com

Performance Diver
P.O. Box 2741
Chapel Hill NC 27514
800-933-2299
Fax 800-727-3291
www.performancediver.com

Travel Providers

Adventure Express
650 5th St.
San Francisco CA 94107
415-442-0709
800-443-0799
Fax 415-442-0289
E-mail: dema@adventureexpress.
   com
www.AdventureExpress.com

Aggressor Fleet Ltd.
7810 Hwy. 90 E.
P.O. Box 1470
Morgan City LA 70381-2814
504-385-2628
800-348-2628
Fax 504-384-0817
E-mail: diveboat@aol.com
www.aggressor.com

Asia Transpacific Divers
3055 Center Green Dr.
Boulder CO 80301
303-443-6789
Fax 303-443-7078
E-mail: info@southeastasia.com
www.southeastasia.com

Bahamas Travel Network
1403 SE 17th St.
Fort Lauderdale FL 33309

954-467-1133
Fax 954-467-7544
E-mail: travel@internetmci.com
www.bahamastravelnet.com

Blackbeard's Cruises
P.O. Box 661091
Miami FL 33166
305-888-1226
800-327-9600
E-mail: sales@blackbeard-
   cruises.com
www.blackbeard-cruises.com

Broadreach (specializes in dive
   trips for teenagers)
P.O. Box 27076
Raleigh NC 27611
888-833-1907
Fax 919-833-2129
E-mail: broadreach@gobroadreach.
   com
www.gobroadreach.com

Club Med
75 Valencia Ave.
Coral Gables FL 33134
305-925-9000
800-CLUB-MED (800-258-2633)
www.clubmed.com

Deep Discoveries
3A 1st Ave. N.
Mulhurst Bay AL
TOC 2CO Canada
800-667-5362
Fax 780-389-4077
E-mail: deepdiscoveries@
   incentre.net
www.deepdiscoveries.com

Dive Discovery
1005 A St., Suite 202
San Rafael CA 94901
800-886-7321
Fax 415-258-9115

E-mail: divetrips@DiveDiscovery.
   com
www.divediscovery.com

Dive Guide International
See under Mail-Order Companies

Dive Travel Services
595 Fairbanks St.
Corona CA 91719
800-544-7631
Fax 909-279-0478
E-mail: travel@scubavoyages.com
www.scubavoyages.com

Experience the Adventure Tours
1350 SW 57th Ave., Suite 315
Miami FL 33144
305-267-6644
Fax 305-261-6648
E-mail: etatours@aol.com
www.empg.com/eta

International Diving Expeditions
18280 Avenida Caleta, Suite 201
Murrieta CA 92562
909-698-3189
800-544-3483
Fax 909-698-3289
E-mail ide@love2travel.com

Island Dreams Travel
8582 Katy Freeway, Suite 118
Houston TX 77024
713-973-9300
800-346-6116
Fax 713-973-8585
E-mail: info@islandream.com
www.islandream.com

PADI Travel Network (referrals
   to tour operators and dive
   operators)
30151 Tomas St.
Rancho Santa Margarita CA
   92688

949-858-7234
800-729-7234
E-mail: trade@padi.com
www.padi.com/PTN/

Peter Hughes Diving, Inc.
1390 S. Dixie Hwy., Suite 1109
Coral Gables FL 33146
305-669-9391
800-932-6237
Fax 305-669-6237
E-mail: dancer@peterhughes.com
www.peterhughes.com

Poseidon Ventures Tours
359 San Miguel Dr.
Newport Beach CA 92660
949-644-5344
E-mail: poseidon@fea.net
www.poseidontours.com

Rascals in Paradise (specialist in
   worldwide family vacations)
650 5th St., Suite 505
San Francisco CA 94107
415-978-9800
800-URASCAL
   (800-872-7225)
Fax 415-442-0289
E-mail: dema@rascalsinparadise.
   com
www.rascalsinparadise.com

SeaLink Corporation (real-time
   reservations system for resorts
   and dive operators)
407 W. Michigan St.
Duluth MN 55802
218-722-8100
Fax 218-722-7672
E-mail: mike@sealinkars.com
www.sealinkars.com

Ticket Planet (specialist in
   discount airfares to dive
   destinations)
59 Grant Ave., Level 3
San Francisco CA 94108
415-288-9999
800-799-8888
Fax 415-288-9839
E-mail: nick@ticketplanet.com
www.ticketplanet.com

Tropical Adventures
111 2nd N.
Seattle WA 98109
206-441-3483
Fax 206-441-5431
E-mail dive@divetropical.com

Ultimate Dive Travel
1329 W. Irving Park Rd.,
   Suite 101
Bensenville IL 60106
630-616-9926

800-737-3483
Fax 620-616-0727
E-mail: udive@flashnet
www.ultimatedivetravel.com

Worlddive and Caribbean
   Adventures
4700 Hiatus Rd., Suite 252
Sunrise FL 33352
800-433-3483
Fax 954-434-4282
E-mail: reservationky@
   worlddive. com
www.worlddive.ky

World Diving Services
4127 5th Ave. N.
St. Petersburg FL 33713-9969
727-321-0187
800-594-6825
Fax 727-388-0223
E-mail: worlddive@aol.com
www.worldive.com

World of Diving and Adventure
   Vacations
301 Main St.
El Segundo CA 90245
310-222-8100
800-GO-DIVING (800-463-4846)
Fax 310-322-5111
E-mail: mail@worldofdiving.com
www.worldofdiving.com

Index